Essential

Retirement

Planning

for Solo Agers

A retirement and aging roadmap for single and childless adults

Sara Zeff Geber, PhD

Founder of LifeEncore

PRAISE FOR *ESSENTIAL RETIREMENT PLANNING FOR SOLO AGERS*

"Sara Zeff Geber's book is a must-read ... not just for solo agers but for anyone looking to have the best aging experience possible. Planning for retirement today has changed dramatically. Boomers are living longer and have the opportunity to embrace new frontiers. Dr. Geber does an excellent job of addressing the concerns and opportunities we encounter as we age."

—Ken Dychtwald, PhD,
Author of A New Purpose: Redefining Money, Family, Work, Retirement, and Success

"Sara Geber provides an excellent, comprehensive guide to aging and covers a wide variety of topics ranging from reinventing yourself to leaving a legacy to making wise long-term care choices. Readers will find her insights very helpful as they chart the second half of their lives."

—Richard Eisenberg,
Managing Editor at *Nextavenue.org*

"When it comes to aging, you can't count on your children, especially if you don't have any. But help is on the way. Sara Geber has given remarkable guidance in her book Solo Agers. You may be solo, but you're not alone. Don't wait to read the book."

—Harry R. Moody, PhD,
Author, Retired Vice President for Academic Affairs, AARP

"Time to take our heads out of the sand. While there is no guarantee that adult children will step in to help financially and with caregiving as their parents age, those of us aging without children are particularly at risk of flying without a net. Geber explores with authority why it's imperative to take the time to plan for our future financial security, social network, and more. We must take a clear-eyed appraisal of what we might require, as the years move along, and who will be on our team to lend a hand and have our backs. At its heart, this solid book is chock-full of straightforward advice and captivating stories to spur the creative conversations today that will allow us to plan for our journey with care and confidence."

—**Kerry Hannon,**
AARP's Job Expert and bestselling author of *Great Jobs for Everyone 50+: Finding Work That Keeps You Happy and Healthy … and Pays the Bills*

"This book fills a void of addressing retirement issues for adults with no children. Yet it is much more. Its message is of value to all of us who want our next chapter of life to be the best one. Sara seamlessly integrates important content about health, fitness, financial security, social connections, and meaning with poignant interviews and self-evaluation exercises. The book feels personal, as though I was having a cup of coffee with the author. The words flow effortlessly. I recommend this to those with or without children who want to create their own best aging experience. Kudos to you, Sara, for your important contribution."

—**Helen Dennis,**
Author, columnist, and lecturer on aging and the new retirement
Co-author of *Project Renewment: The First Retirement Model for Career Women*

"In Essential Retirement Planning for Solo Agers, Sara reminds us that aging alone doesn't have to be a scary proposition, and it also doesn't

mean living in isolation. By establishing our social networks and building communities through house sharing and other alternative living options, we can create our own nurturing support systems designed to help us thrive socially and financially in our retirement years. This information-packed guide has valuable insights to help everyone architect successful retirement solutions, but particularly for those who will be 'Solo Aging.'"

—Wendi Burkhardt,
Silvernest CEO & Founder

"Planners—this book is for you! Procrastinators—run, don't walk to get your copy of this practical, information-rich, and inspiring guide."

—Betsy Werley,
Encore.org, Director of Network Expansion

"While most older people are not lonely, gerontologists know that those without children are at greater risk for loneliness and isolation. Dr. Sara Geber's practical, readable guide, based on solid scientific research, is a much-needed planning resource for 'solo agers' and the gerontologists who work with them."

—Donna E. Schafer, PhD, CPG,
Executive Director, National Association for Professional Gerontologists

"Aging is a challenge, even under the best of circumstances. As we get older, we all have to deal with inevitable losses and increasing health risks. In this country, children are expected to provide care for their elders, but this is often problematic for those who are aging on their own without traditional support. Sara Geber has written an encouraging guide to those who are 'aging solo' and shows how they can make sure that they, too, have the resources and connections they need to thrive in later life."

—Richard Adler,
Distinguished Fellow, *Institute for the Future*

"Thank you, Dr. Sara Zeff Geber, for giving me a solid roadmap with all the essential planning tools to implement while aging alone. I have no partner or adult children to count on for support and help, and the predicament concerns me. But the tools in Dr. Geber's (your) book, Essential Retirement Planning for Solo Agers, empower me to design a well-though-out retirement plan to remain safe, independent, and financially secure, and to age well at home. I appreciate your wisdom, advice, and knowledge. I'm so happy you put it all together for individuals like me."

—Carol Marak,
Aging Alone advocate, founder of the *Elder Orphan* Facebook group,
editor at Seniorcare.com.

"As the baby boomers age, society is faced with a growing population of those who are aging alone. This book serves as a guide to help you plan and strategize for a stage of life we may all one day face. Sara Geber methodically outlines the areas we should focus on that will enable us to promote our own longevity and independence."

—Maria Carney, MD

"This pioneering, beautifully written book will change the way you see and think about retirement. It opens our eyes to the emergence of an entirely *new positive life stage of solo aging. Solo or not, read this most important book to live your retirement life with purpose."*

—**Richard Leider,**
International bestselling author of *The Power of Purpose, Repacking Your Bags,* and *Life Reimagined*

"Sara Geber's well-written book for those who are aging solo is a treasure trove of good advice and terrific resources for people who can't count on adult children as a safety net. The stories sprinkled throughout the book illustrate how other Solo Agers have prepared for their retirement and created their own safety net for aging, and the worksheets and checklists provide a painless aid to the planning process."

—**Hyrum Smith,**
Author of bestselling *Purposeful Retirement*

"Sara Geber's book has arrived not a moment too soon—not only for me, but for the millions of others who are solo agers. Although I do think that all older adults will benefit from the breadth and depth of the information contained within its pages. In addition to running my PR agency, I serve on my city's Human Services Commission (we are a member of the age-friendly cities network), on my County's Commission for Older Adults and on a state-level Livable Communities Advisory Team. I cannot wait to share Dr. Geber's extraordinary book with these organizations and their stakeholders."

—**Barbara Meltzer,**
Barbara Meltzer & Associates, Public Relations and Marketing

Essential Retirement Planning for Solo Agers

Essential Retirement Planning for Solo Agers

A Retirement and Aging Roadmap for Single and Childless Adults

Sara Zeff Geber, PhD

Mango Publishing

Coral Gables, FL

For permission requests, please contact the publisher at:
Mango Publishing Group
2850 Douglas Road, 3rd Floor
Coral Gables, FL 33134 USA
info@mango.bz

For special orders, quantity sales, course adoptions and corporate sales, please email the publisher at sales@mango.bz. For trade and wholesale sales, please contact Ingram Publisher Services at customer.service@ingramcontent.com or +1.800.509.4887.

Essential Retirement Planning for Solo Agers: A Retirement and Aging Roadmap for Single and Childless Adults

Library of Congress Cataloging-in-Publication has been applied for.
ISBN: (p) 978-1-63353-768-2 (e) 978-1-63353-769-9
BISAC category code BUS050040 BUSINESS & ECONOMICS / Personal Finance / Retirement Planning

Printed in the United States of America

This book is dedicated to my husband, Charles "Chuck" Geber. His belief in my ability to produce this book has been unwavering, as has his support and encouragement. He has been my sounding board and a willing reader and editor throughout the process.

Table of Contents

PART III: DECIDING HOW AND WHERE TO LIVE

PART IV: ENSURING COMFORT AND CARE IN YOUR OLDEST AGE

FOREWORD

This book is for you. Don't say you're not a Solo Ager. The truth is, we're all Solo Agers if we live long enough. Successful Solo Agers have learned how to age alone and they have lessons we all need to learn. This book will give you those lessons.

WAIT! Before you put down this page and get into the book, think a bit about what I've just said and take it seriously.

I'm a seventy-three-year-old gerontologist who's moving, by inches, into old age. I wrote a textbook in gerontology, but I learned more from personal example than I ever did from books. I had the great good fortune, with my wife, to spend seven years caring for our dear friend Larry Morris, who moved into our home and later died in our midst at the age of ninety-seven. As Larry approached his nineties, he had outlived two wives and had no children. He was a Solo Ager and his example remains an inspiration to me.

In the classic novel *Goodbye, Mr. Chips*, the hero is a man who has spent his life as a humble teacher at a boys' school. He's lying on his deathbed when he overhears friends talking about his life, saying it was a pity he never had any children. Mr. Chips pipes up to say "But you're wrong. I have! Thousands of 'em, thousands of 'em ... and all ... boys."

Mr. Chips has spent his life as what we might call an investor in social capital: in the "ties that bind" us together and that make our lives meaningful in the end. Successful Solo Agers are those who have done best at cultivating those ties. That's the lesson I learned from Larry Morris, who spent so many years of his life giving to others and cultivating friends, including younger friends, like me and my wife.

The Beatles had it down when they sang, "I get by with a little help from my friends." Those lyrics sound like a cliché, but they aren't. Epidemiologists are now discovering that isolation and loneliness constitute "the new smoking." The lack of social ties has a devastating impact on mortality and life expectancy. In short, "going it alone" can kill you. Successful Solo Agers are those who are solo only in certain respects. They are the successful investors in social capital, and this book will show you how to learn from what they already know.

So, whether married or single, childless or with children, we all have to ask the question: Can we learn to be an "investor in social capital?" Yes, we can. Sociological theorists like Robert Putnam (*Bowling Alone*) can tell you how to do it. As with physical health, when it comes to strengthening social ties, it's never too late to make up for lost time— and in our overly busy world we all have to struggle against that threat of lost time. Prof. Putnam has warned us about the dangers, as a society, of depleting our social capital. It's up to us to take that warning seriously.

My wife of forty-eight years and I have two grown children, a son and daughter in their thirties, so perhaps we don't technically qualify as a "Solo Agers." But maybe I should say "not yet." The truth is, as I said earlier, eventually, one member of a couple dies before the other. On a statistical basis, bereavement affects women more than men, but I have more than one close male friend who's a widower.

Take seriously the idea that you, like me, may one day be a Solo Ager. Never think, as the friends of Mr. Chips did, that it's a pity you never had any children. Instead, read what this book has to offer and don't delay a single day in applying its lessons.

—Harry R. Moody, PhD,
Visiting Professor, Fielding Graduate School,
Retired Vice President for Academic Affairs, AARP

Harry "Rick" Moody is the author of over 100 scholarly articles, as well as numerous books on aging. Dr. Moody previously served as Executive Director of the Brookdale Center on Aging at Hunter College and was Chairman of the Board of Elderhostel (now Road Scholar).

His new book, Gerontology: The Basics, will be published by Routledge in 2017. In 2011, he received the Lifetime Achievement Award from the American Society on Aging; in 2010, Masterpiece Living honored him with the Robert Kahn Award for Successful Aging; and in 2008 he was named by Utne Reader Magazine as one of "50 Visionaries Who Are Changing Your World."

CHAPTER 1. INTRODUCTION

About six years ago, I started noticing that many of my friends were spending a lot of time tending to aging parents. Those who lived nearby were needed for driving, relocation, managing medications, bringing them to doctor's appointments. Those whose parent(s) lived further away did their caregiving long distance—by managing local caregivers or by spending a lot of time on airplanes. None of my friends had thought about this ahead of time, and neither had their parents. But suddenly mom fell or a doctor called to say that dad shouldn't drive anymore or mom's behavior had become worrisome.

These friends of mine, these adult children were called in to help, no matter their history of closeness or off-again on-again estrangement. They showed up. Who else would do it? If there were other siblings, they usually shared the responsibility and the tasks, those living closest carrying the lion's share, with expenses divvied up among them as best they could be.

One day, my friend Monica told me about her recent visit with her ninety-two-year-old father-in-law. She had been flying from California to upstate New York several times a year for the past three years, staying for three to four weeks at a time. During her visits she made sure he was keeping his house in order, preparing nutritious meals for himself, and paying his bills. She talked to the neighbors, went to church with him, and restocked the pantry to reassure herself and her husband that he was healthy and safe.

However, now she was concerned. On her most recent visit, Edward was displaying some troubling behaviors. He was not keeping up with his personal hygiene, and he had started wandering through the house in the middle of the night. A couple of times, thinking it was morning, he prepared breakfast for the two of them at three in the morning. Monica and her husband decided it was time to look for a residential facility and start the difficult task of preparing him for the move. Since her husband had a full-time job, they decided Monica would stay in New York for an additional month, keeping an eye on her father-in-law and managing the "project."

When I hung up the phone and thought about what she had just told me, I asked myself, "*Who will do that for us?*" The answer "*No one*" made me gasp.

My husband and I are in our sixties and have no children. We are professionals with a lot of education and serious careers, like many of our friends—people who used to be called "DINKs" (double income, no kids). As I dug deeper, I discovered a 2005 Pew Research study which reported that 19.4 percent of the boomer generation did not have kids (almost *double* the percentage of child-free women in all previous generations).[1] Wow!

Who will do for us what we did for our parents?

With the *natural* infertility rate among women around 10 percent, it seemed odd that the baby boomer rate was so high. Then it dawned on me that there were a couple of logical reasons. Number one, the baby boomers were the first generation to arrive at adolescence *after* the introduction of the birth control pill. The second reason is that baby boomer women were the first truly liberated women in United States history. Higher education was available, the US legal system made it a crime to discriminate on the basis of gender, and by 1980, women had begun challenging every male stronghold. A boomer woman no longer

---

1   Pew Research Center, Childlessness Falls, Family Size Grows Among Highly Educated Women (Washington, DC: May 2015). Available at http://www. pewsocialtrends.org/2015/05/07/childlessness-falls-family-size-grows-among-highly-educated-women/. The 19.4 percent statistic is from the second section, "Childlessness," available at http://www.pewsocialtrends.org/2015/05/07/childlessness/.

needed a man to support her. She could remain single for life or put off marriage until her thirties or forties.

Sometime in my thirties, I made a conscious choice to NOT have children. Have I ever regretted that choice? Occasionally, but only in recent years as I listen to my friends talk about their special relationships with their grandkids. On the other hand, it's pretty hard to conjure up a relationship with grandkids when I never had kids!

If I had it to do over again, I would make the same choices. I continue to enjoy a life enriched by a challenging and ever-changing career, wonderful friends, travel, hobbies I enjoy, continuous learning, and a solid relationship with a spouse who shares my love of music, my political leanings, and most of my food preferences. We continue to fill our lives with canine companions and good friends, many of whom are also child-free baby boomers. Some of them have close ties with nieces and nephews—and as you will see in Part III, that can be very helpful in advance planning.

I wrote this book for those who live alone or, for whatever reason, have no adult children. Whether you are married/partnered or single in the second half of life (over fifty) you will not have the safety net of that immediate younger generation to count on later in life in an emergency or even an extended illness.

I do not have children, and everything I recommend in this book I have undertaken myself. These pages include many stories of others like me (whose names have been changed) from all over the country who are blazing new trails and making creative choices appropriate to their own unique circumstances. I hope my stories, research, experience, and observations encourage you to begin the planning necessary for peace of mind as you age. The journey is not long, complicated, or unnecessarily expensive. If your financial resources are slim, you may need to be creative or ask for help. Most of all, I hope this will lead you to begin a conversation with your family and friends about what you want your future to look like and the role you would like them to play.

PART I

PREPARING FOR THE FUTURE

Chapter 2. Child-Free: Pioneers of a Generation

"Sandra Day O'Connor and Ruth Bader Ginsburg paved the way for me and so many other women in my generation. Their pioneering lives have created boundless possibilities for women in the law ..."

—Elena Kagan, Supreme Court Justice

Congratulations! You are a pioneer of your generation. You have successfully navigated your life along an unconventional path. Most child-free adults made a deliberate choice not to have children. Although that decision was somewhat more acceptable for baby boomers than for previous generations, most boomer women—and men—continued to experience a great deal of pressure to marry and raise families. If you held fast against those pressures, you demonstrated strength in your convictions. You deserve to be proud of your accomplishments and the path you chose.

I interviewed a large number of women and a few men—all child-free—for this book. They shared their stories with me about their choice to not raise children and where their lives had taken them. Some had led conventional lives; some had cast caution to the wind and chosen more varied and exciting lifestyles. Because they did not have children dependent on them, they had had more options—changing careers on a whim, moving to a different state or country, or experimenting with alternative lifestyles.

The women I interviewed never felt compelled to be mothers; they were drawn to other occupations and interests. In the late 1970s, women who wanted to be mothers described their maternal urge as the ticking of their "biological clocks." I never experienced that internal pressure, nor did the child-free women I interviewed.

Deborah's story provides a good illustration of a boomer woman who chose a solo life:

Born in a suburb of Philadelphia, Deborah attended a local university, majoring in liberal arts with a minor in business, and then getting an advanced degree in organizational studies. She wanted to see more of the country and, with nothing tying her to Pennsylvania, she moved around quite a bit, seeking opportunities to have the active, outdoor lifestyle she loved. She was never particularly career-driven, but as a woman with a master's degree in the 1970s, she had enough education to find good jobs wherever she went.

Deborah ultimately settled far away from her family. She discovered the West Coast had more accessible year-round activities, along with the arts and a diversity of people she came to appreciate. After living for short periods in Southern California, Northern California, and the Portland, Oregon, area, at age thirty-seven she settled in Seattle. By then, she had established a career in human resources and managed to find jobs in her field wherever she landed. In Seattle, she worked first for Boeing, then for the newcomer to the area, Microsoft.

Deborah never felt the urge to marry or have children. She loved being on her own, able to make her own choices, go where she wanted, when she wanted, and with whom she wanted. She had boyfriends along the way, but none of her relationships ever got serious enough to consider marriage. Her independence always came first. Over three decades in Seattle, Deborah developed a strong cadre of friends, mostly other women in her field—some single, some married—with similar interests and experiences. They shared meals, holidays, travel, career ups and downs, and the occasional heartbreak.

At age sixty-three, Deborah looks back at her life as a series of deliberate choices. She continues to enjoy success and fulfillment in her career and her social sphere. She has no immediate plans to quit working, and since becoming a human resources consultant she can now take on as many or as few clients as she chooses.

Having chosen to not have children, you are among the many baby boomer men and women who have created a very different life, one that focused more on achievement and independence than on raising a family. You chose to be an engineer, a flight attendant, a nurse, a doctor, a lawyer, an artist, a builder, or any of the hundreds of professions that were starting to open up to *both* men and women in the 1970s. In choosing not to be a parent, you helped write the story of those like us all over the world. As you crest midlife, you have another opportunity to be a pioneer. This time in the interest of having a safe and secure future as you move into your later decades.

"In every single thing you do, you are choosing a direction. Your life is a product of choices."

—Dr. Kathleen Hall

Always a generation enamored with reinventing itself and the world, baby boomers are now poised to create new ways for living safe, productive, and meaningful lives. Today we are seeing the beginning of new and different community structures, innovative technologies for working when and where we want, and new technologies for living in a more connected way. These developments carry tremendous promise for leading interesting and rewarding lives in our seventies, eighties, nineties, and beyond.

Our later decades of life will differ in important ways from people who have children. We will all face issues common to aging: our own aging parents, personal health challenges, and a gradually slowing pace. However, there are *benefits* to getting older: we are more patient, we see things in shades of gray rather than black and white, and we are no longer novices at our work—we are the experts. And let's not forget about those "senior" discounts. In short, for most people, getting older represents a mixed bag, and we would do well to remember the positives when we are being inundated with the negatives.

The stories of child-free baby boomers are quite varied, yet most revolve around the common themes of independence and freedom. Many of their lives have taken unique twists and turns, owing to the choices they were able to make. In the following stories, Carolyn, Glenn, and Marion are representative of millions of boomers who took full advantage of the opportunities open to them. Their stories give us additional examples of how many child-free people have led their lives:

Carolyn and Glenn are a classic baby boomer couple. Carolyn was born in 1954, the oldest of four siblings in a military family. As her father, a naval officer, moved from base to base every four years, the family accompanied him. That meant Carolyn and her siblings bounced from school to school, never setting down roots in any one place. During her sophomore year in high school, her father retired and the family settled in Fort Collins, a midsize town in Colorado, where her father had secured a teaching position.

The years of rootlessness taught Carolyn how to make friends quickly and find her place in a variety of social situations. Those skills proved valuable in college and beyond. Thinking she might teach, Carolyn majored in English Literature, but teaching didn't suit her. She preferred writing, and from her first job as a newsroom runner, she knew journalism was the right path for her.

Glenn, a year younger, took over his father's insurance business the year he graduated from Colorado State University and discovered that with hard work he could grow it well beyond what his father had achieved. Having been a child of working parents, he had a feel for the stress that accompanied raising children and tending a career at the same time. Glenn had no strong desire to be a father, and when he met Carolyn, he quickly came to understand that her primary interest in life was her journalism career, not motherhood. Glenn and Carolyn both saw their relationship as a good fit. When they got around to talking about marriage and the future, they decided together that they would not raise a family.

After they wed, Glenn told Carolyn that if she had a change of heart about having children, he was open to reconsidering the matter. Carolyn deeply appreciated his willingness to be flexible. From time to time she asked herself whether she was still content not to have children, and the answer kept coming up "yes." In her mid-thirties, she listened to many of her old high school and college friends talking about the ticking of their biological clocks. Carolyn could not discern any such clock inside of her and felt quite satisfied with the work that continued to interest her and the promotions that were rolling her way.

During her thirties and forties, Carolyn worked for a series of daily newspapers, each one larger than the last, and, at age forty-three, became a key editor for one of Colorado's largest dailies. During that same time period, Glenn quadrupled his father's insurance business. He opened three more offices around the state, and when his father retired Glenn assumed the reins of the entire enterprise. When they weren't working, Glenn and Carolyn spent time with extended family, an eclectic assortment of friends from their neighborhood, their respective work circles, and old college chums who were still in the area.

Marion, now sixty-two and a successful marketing executive for a large public relations firm, always loved children and assumed she would marry and start a family sometime after college. However, life didn't go quite as she had planned. Although she grew up in a vibrant, midsize city in Massachusetts, Marion always wanted to see the Northwest, and college gave her that opportunity. Accepted to the University of Washington in Spokane in 1973, she made her way across the country. During Marion's sophomore year, her mother developed metastatic breast cancer. Marion rushed back to Massachusetts to be at her mother's side for the surgery and the chemotherapy that followed.

For the first three years after surgery, her mother responded to treatment, and after six months in Massachusetts, Marion returned to college to finish her degree. Upon graduation, she accepted a marketing job in Tacoma, Washington, and signed a lease on a condominium a few miles from her workplace. Within a year of moving to Tacoma, Marion also fell in love with a man she met through a friend and became engaged to marry. Life appeared to be working out much as she had hoped.

However, in 1980, Marion's mother had a setback and needed more extensive chemotherapy. This time, Marion and her mother decided to pursue further treatment in Washington State so Marion could be with her fiancé and continue working at the job she loved. He helped her sell the Massachusetts home and move her mother into an apartment in Tacoma, about a mile from Marion.

As her mother's treatment became more and more debilitating, Marion found herself going daily, after work, to her mother's apartment to visit and care for her. She did all the shopping and meal preparation as well as helping her mother bathe and dress. On weekends she did her mother's wash as well as her own household chores. The all-consuming job of being her mother's caregiver lasted three full years.

33

During that time, Marion's fiancé felt neglected, and was emotionally disturbed by the cancer. He finally broke off the engagement and walked out of Marion's life.

After three years, Marion's mother fell and broke her hip. Because she needed strength to heal the broken bone, the chemotherapy treatments had to be stopped. However, those treatments were all that had kept the cancer at bay and once they were discontinued the cancer raged anew.

When her mother died, Marion, at thirty, was emotionally and physically exhausted. But as the weeks went by, her body and spirit healed and she rededicated herself to her work. The job began to require quite a bit of travel, limiting Marion's ability to meet another potential marriage partner. However, the fulfillment she found at work more than compensated for the loss of that prospect. She considered having children out of wedlock and raising them herself, but with her demanding job, raising children didn't seem to be a realistic plan and she abandoned the idea. Instead, Marion continued to travel and enjoy the benefits her high-profile job afforded. As she thinks about winding down her career now at sixty-two, she has no regrets about how she pursued her life and how things turned out for her.

The life path for most child-free baby boomers has depended on several factors. Among more educated women with higher-paying jobs, being without children at midlife has meant more freedom to come and go at will, living alone or with a companion of their choice. Single or married, they have established social networks that include a personalized mixture of friends and blood relatives. Men have followed similar paths, but theirs have typically relied more on work-related networks and connections and less on contact with family members.

A growing number of men and women today, regardless of age, are *choosing* to remain single for life. The age at first marriage is now in the upper twenties for both men and women, and appears to rise every year. In the United States today, as in much of Western Europe, one hundred million people—almost 50 percent of the population over eighteen—report as "single" in the census rolls.[2] Some unmarried women now raise children they have adopted or birthed, but among baby boomers the majority of single people remain child-free, especially men.

"Conservative estimates suggest that there are more than 3 million LGBT people age fifty-five and older in the US—1.5 million of whom are sixty-five and older. This over-sixty-five segment will double in the next few decades as millions of Americans enter retirement age. Unfortunately, due to a lifetime of discrimination, many LGBT people age without proper community supports, in poor health, and financially insecure."

—Advocacy & Services for LGBT Elders (sageusa.org)

A very large proportion of the LGBT community does not have children. Around twenty percent have kids, either from previous heterosexual relationships, or through adoption or artificial insemination, but the majority of LGBT boomers do not have children.[3] Today, same-sex couples are legally allowed to marry, and those unions are becoming increasingly accepted in society. This acceptance has opened the doors for more parenting among gay couples, either

2   "Facts for Features: Unmarried and Single Americans Week Sept. 21-27, 2014," US Census Bureau, Release Number: CB14-FF.21, http://www.census.gov/newsroom/facts-for-features/2014/cb14-ff21.html/.

3   Gary Gates, "Family Formation and Raising Children among Same-Sex Couples," National Council on Family Relations Report Family Focus 51 (Winter 2011), F1-F4. Available at https://williamsinstitute.law.ucla.edu/wp-content/uploads/Gates-Badgett-NCFR-LGBT-Families-December-2011.pdf.

through adoption or surrogacy. However, most gay men and women in prior generations are child-free, like Ken:

Ken, born in Cleveland in 1938, went to private schools and an eastern college, then to the University of Michigan Law School, as a good background for politics.

After graduation, he joined a small firm in a midsize Northern Michigan city, and was soon elected to the state legislature. After three terms, he decided he would be happier in the executive branch of state government. He then worked in the governor's office for five more years before burning out on politics altogether. He felt adrift, not only with regard to his career, but also his sexual orientation. He knew his life had to change in some fundamental ways.

Ken took a year off, and then went into teaching at a Michigan law school. He dated women off and on, but never let the relationships get serious. At thirty-nine, he decided he needed to explore, once and for all, whether he preferred men. On a winter break, he went to Key West, Florida, where the gay lifestyle was already openly happening.

Ken returned to Michigan sure of his preference for men, and began to discreetly explore the gay scene in the town where he taught, which proved to be both frightening and unsatisfactory. He returned to school for a master's degree, then landed a teaching job at a college in Miami.

Life was better for Ken in Florida, with its larger cities and greater opportunities for self-expression, including sexual preference. He developed a deep and devoted relationship with a man. Both in their mid-forties, they discussed the possibility of adopting children but decided they were too old to start a family. Now retired from teaching, Ken lives in Key West, where he remains active, working to integrate the gay and lesbian communities into the larger population.

Those of us that are child-free may be married, divorced, widowed, or single. We come in all colors and represent a wide variety of backgrounds, but all of us need to prepare for our later years without the help of adult children. That's what makes us unique. Today's outlook for the senior years promises many choices—for parents as well as non-parents.

When asked about options for a rewarding older adulthood in the early twenty-first century, I like to say, "This is not your father's retirement!"

We still fear the big three health challenges, but most people now survive heart attacks and strokes and can live for years, even decades, after cancer treatment. Life expectancy across the United States has been increasing steadily and now hovers in the early- to mid-eighties, so we must stay as healthy and positive as we can in order to enjoy what gerontologists Lynn Peters Adler, Ken Dychtwald, and others have called "the bonus years."

Jean Houston, teacher, author, and leadership guru for the United Nations, calls this stage of life "the great turning point."[4] She goes on to suggest that we "don't know a darn thing till we are about fifty-five or sixty. The years after that are the years in which you can bring your humanity to bear upon the great issues of our time." She includes, in this new way of thinking about older age, the pursuit of lifelong education—both learning and teaching—and reminds us that we have lived through more history of the human race than our grandparents could ever have imagined. Wow! What a positive way to think about our post-fifty lives.

"Life without a script" provides another way of looking at these bonus years. Specific expectations were at play for all earlier stages of life. Here's how the life script reads: from ages one through five,

---

4   Jean Houston, "The Journey of Transformation," in Audacious Aging, ed. S. Marohn (Santa Rosa, CA: Elite Books, 2008), 161-66.

we are in strong growth mode. We are learning how to get from one place to another in our environment. We are learning about rules and danger and how to express ourselves. Our "job" at that time of life is learning about our separateness from the others around us. Once we enter school, our role is to learn, to achieve, and to earn rewards. We also have to learn social skills during that time. We have to navigate the waters of love, indifference, and hatred, and resolve complicated relationship and sexual questions. And we have to cut the ties with our parents. Once out of school we have to learn to live on our own and support ourselves. Most people's scripts include finding a partner and, for many, starting a family. For those without children, the next part of the script involves nurturing our careers and pursuing activities that are interesting and fulfilling.

This last part of the script takes us up to around age fifty-five or sixty, at which time the script ends. What now? In American society, the script ends when we leave our careers. For parents, a partial script exists, which involves being a grandparent. However, the main actors in that production are the younger parents themselves, so grandparents play a supporting role at best, unless the parents are incapacitated or unavailable.

Most of us age in stages. If you are reading this book, you are probably in the early stages of older adulthood: fifty-five to seventy. In those years, statistics are on your side. Many people today live healthy lives well into their seventies and eighties, in fact, more and more people are aging to triple digits every year. However, 70 percent of us will need some level of assistance to manage our lives,[5] especially as we get into our mid to late eighties and beyond. None of us knows in advance how much or what kind of assistance we will need.

---

5   "How Much Care Will You Need?," last modified October 10, 2017, US Department of Health and Human Services Website, https://longtermcare.acl.gov/the-basics/how-much-care-will-you-need.html.

Another mystery is how long we will live. Many factors are at play: general health, genetics, lifestyle, habits, stress tolerance, and more. Because of this uncertainty, we can't know for sure how much money we will need to fund that long life. Planning requires us to make some educated guesses and prepare for uncertain times.

In the following chapters you will meet more child-free people who have taken the reins of their lives and made plans for their future happiness and safety in a variety of ways. Some have chosen to continue working long past the typical retirement age; some have chosen unique lifestyles and living environments; some have chosen new community designs. Indeed, there is no end in sight to the creative ways those of us without children can prepare for our remaining years.

In addition, we will need to give thought and make plans for how to receive care in our oldest years. In later chapters you will meet child-free people who have made those plans—some in conventional ways, others in brave new ways. They have all done their homework and followed their hearts. I found their stories fascinating and encouraging. They spurred me to do the additional research to round out the guidance offered in these pages. If you take the stories and recommendations to heart and plan aggressively for your later years, you will be able to sit back and continue to enjoy the same freedom you have had all your life. Enjoy the ride!

CHAPTER 3. THE ROLE OF ADULT CHILDREN IN THE LIFE OF AN ELDER

"Blood relatives have always been the only source of morally obligated support in later life."

—Robert Rubenstein, Social Scientist

Let me start this chapter by telling you the story of Fred and Hildy, a couple without children who did not plan for their later years, but got very lucky at the end. My colleague and friend, Andrea Gallagher, shared their story with me and offered to let me use their real names. She and her husband Peter, who do not themselves have children, learned some great lessons from it ... and so did I.

Hildy and Fred in their home in 2005

Andrea and Peter had recently moved into a new home and invited a few of their closest neighbors over to introduce themselves. Fred, eighty-six, and Hildy, eighty-nine, were the oldest couple on the block, having lived in their home since the neighborhood was developed, over forty years earlier. They arrived at the party a little early and stayed throughout.

As they got to know Fred and Hildy better, Peter and Andrea started helping them with small chores like putting up holiday decorations. They also learned Fred and Hildy had no children and no close relatives. Early one Saturday morning, about eighteen months later, Hildy called and asked if one of them could take Fred to the hospital for a minor procedure. Hildy did not drive. She was mostly wheelchair-bound because of macular degeneration and crippling arthritis in her legs.

What was to be a quick outpatient surgery for Fred turned into a weeklong stay at the hospital. Frustrated and concerned about the turn of events, Fred asked Andrea and Peter to sleep over at his house so Hildy would not be afraid. How could they say no? Every day they took Hildy to see Fred and either Peter or Andrea stayed with Hildy each night. One of those nights Hildy came down the hall in her motorized chair at three o'clock in the morning, fully dressed, and announced she wanted to "take you kids to breakfast."

After a week, Fred was able to leave the hospital and return home. At about that point, it became clear to Andrea and Peter that Fred had been acting as a caregiver to Hildy in recent years as she became more and more disabled, both mentally and physically. Many other neighbors shared their relief that Peter and Andrea "came along" when they did. They had all known Fred and Hildy would need help, and no one knew who was going to help them.

Andrea and Peter began to prepare meals, take them to doctor appointments, and over time saw both of them through several more of Fred's hospital stays. Over the next few years, watching over Hildy and Fred became part of Andrea and Peter's lives. With the help of an aide, they oversaw all of the older couple's daily needs.

When Hildy was medically confirmed with dementia, Fred was devastated. They had been married for sixty-three years and his life partner was slipping away before his eyes. A few months later, Fred developed sepsis and ended up in intensive care fighting for his life. Upon recovering from that episode, he recognized that he and Hildy could no longer depend solely on each other for their safety and well-being. He asked Andrea and Peter to be their legal agents, with permission to take over medical and financial decision-making for both of them, and ultimately to be executors of their wills. This was a huge responsibility, yet they felt honored to be able to help these two people they had grown to love.

Hildy died in 2009, and Fred, a year and five days later. Peter and Andrea often tell people of how they "adopted" their elderly neighbors and, though they were often overwhelmed by the work it entailed, they were glad to have been there to help avert a crisis.

Fred and Hildy were extremely lucky to find, at the eleventh hour, two trustworthy and caring people. We can all imagine what might have happened to them had Andrea and Peter not been so charitable and accommodating, or if they had seen their vulnerable neighbors as easy prey and taken advantage of a chance to siphon funds from their accounts or, worse yet, been abusive in their treatment of them.

Thankfully, the story of Hildy and Fred had a happy ending as well as an added bonus: Andrea and Peter learned, through their relationship with Fred and Hildy, that intergenerational relationships are one of the keys to survival for those without children. The experience motivated them to expand their social sphere to include people of many ages, and spurred them to do some additional planning for their own future.

What else can be gleaned from the story of Fred and Hildy? They were "aging in place" and they went into crisis. Their story gets repeated over and over, throughout cities and towns across America. Aging in place is a crapshoot. You may do well for a long time, but things can go downhill very quickly. When the body or mind of an aging parent deteriorates to the point where they endanger themselves by living alone, an adult child usually steps in to help them make a change. Those of us without children need to anticipate the possibility of this kind of trajectory and prepare others to step in when we need help and care.

Having children has never provided a guarantee of emotional and physical support in later life. However, as social scientist Robert Rubinstein and others have concluded from their research, "blood relatives have always been the only source of morally obligated support in later life."[6] That's a strong and sobering statement. As the baby boomer generation moves into the later decades of life, those of us without children will need to take a hard look at what we might need and who will be there to help us.

Studying what adult children today are doing for their aging parents is an excellent way to better understand our potential needs in later life. Mary's story gives us a good example of some of the ways adult children are assisting their aging parents, and demonstrates the complicated emotions involved, the creativity required, and the time-consuming nature of the support role:

> Mary, who is sixty-three, has a ninety-three-year-old mother, Virginia, who still lives in the two-story house in which Mary grew up. Mary, however, has a good job and many friends in another state and has no plans to uproot her life to move back to her hometown. Although they are on good terms today, Mary and Virginia had a somewhat rocky relationship in the past, and vestiges of the old animosity remain.

---

6   Robert L. Rubinstein, Baine B. Alexander, Marchene Goodman, Mark Luborsky, Baine B. Alexander, Marcene Goodman, and Mark Luborsky, "Key Relationships of Never Married, Childless Older Women: A Cultural Analysis," Journal of Gerontology 46(5) (September 1991): 270-77.

When Virginia was in her late eighties, Mary tried to convince her to sell the large family home and move into a retirement community, but Virginia was unwilling to move. Mary visits as often as her demanding job will allow, but her trips are still fewer than once a month.

About five years ago, Mary was able to convince her mother to pay for some modifications to her home. Mary and Virginia interviewed contractors together, ultimately hiring a local construction company to enlarge a bathroom, install grab bars, erect a ramp from the front door to the street level walkway, and reinforce a railing on the interior stairs. Virginia insisted that climbing the stairs to her bedroom each night was "good exercise," and Mary was unable to convince her otherwise.

As an alternative to more frequent visits, Mary has taught her mother to use Skype on her computer. Mary and her mother talk several times a week, and Skype allows Mary to monitor her mother's facial expressions, general pallor, and get a glimpse of the kitchen where Virginia keeps her computer. Mary always asks to see the pill bottles and watches her mother take her medication.

Though still mentally sharp, Virginia knows she doesn't do as good a job managing her financial affairs as she once did, so she allows Mary to help her remotely once a month. They go online together and pay the bills on the bank's website. This generally takes them about an hour because Virginia has lots of questions and tends to forget from one month to the next how the system works.

Mary and Virginia share a financial advisor and Virginia has grudgingly given her consent to allow Mary to speak to the professional about both accounts. However, Virginia is still reluctant to give Mary full access to her finances, so there are aspects of Virginia's life Mary knows nothing about.

To Mary's great relief, Virginia has remained active in her church and in her bridge club. Members of both groups visit her regularly and often bring her food she can heat and eat for several days. Mary has also arranged for a young woman to come in three times a week to do some light housekeeping.

Similar stories are playing out everywhere today with parents who are aging in their homes and in retirement communities with limited services. Even in residential care communities, substantial involvement by adult children is evident. In 2010, a national study found 90 percent of men and women in nursing homes and assisted living communities experienced regular and frequent visits by loved ones.[7] The casual observer in a nursing home or assisted living community can see immediately that these visits are overwhelmingly from children and grandchildren. Adult children play a significant role in the lives of their aging parents. In fact, adult children are sometimes the ONLY source of emotional support available to the aging parent, especially one who has isolated himself or herself from community contacts or has a life-limiting disease.

Lisa's mother, Alice, was diagnosed with Alzheimer's disease when she was seventy-four. Since Lisa's father had died two years earlier and her brother was a barely functioning alcoholic, Lisa was left to see her mother through the debilitating disease. For a couple of years, Alice lived on her own in a large, age-restricted mobile home park in Palm Springs. She had long-time friends and neighbors there who checked on her and reported back to Lisa if there was a problem. Lisa was a three-hour drive away, so she and her mother stayed in touch by phone.

7   G. Khatutsky et al., Residential Care Communities and Their Residents in 2010: A National Portrait (DHHS Publication No. 2016-1041; Hyattsville, MD: National Center for Health Statistics, 2016). Available at https://www.cdc.gov/nchs/data/nsrcf/nsrcf_chartbook.pdf.

After those first two years, Lisa grew increasingly uneasy with her mother's living alone, especially since Alice was no longer driving and had to depend on friends for rides to doctor appointments and shopping. Lisa found herself spending most weekends in Palm Springs. The six-hour round-trip was exhausting and took a toll on Lisa's own family and job.

The following spring, Lisa decided to move Alice into assisted living with memory care in Palm Springs. She used the proceeds from the sale of her mother's mobile home to finance the move. Lisa chose to keep her mother in familiar surroundings and near her doctors rather than move her closer to her own home in suburban Los Angeles. However, the move further isolated Alice from her old friends and neighbors, which put Lisa front and center as the only support person in her mother's life.

Although she knew her mother was safe in assisted living, Lisa continued to spend most weekends in Palm Springs, taking Alice out for meals, supplying her with her favorite snacks, picking up medications, buying her clothing and shoes, and talking to her about things she was still able to remember from the past.

After five years, the round-trip journey became too hard, both emotionally and physically. Lisa finally made the decision to move her mother once more, this time to an assisted living facility nearer to her own home.

Today, Lisa is sixty-five and Alice is eighty-eight. After fourteen years with the disease, Alice no longer recognizes Lisa, but that hasn't stopped Lisa from visiting, staying in touch with her doctors, and checking with the staff in the memory care unit to find out what her mother needs. Lisa has had her own health challenges to deal with, which have limited her ability to visit her mother as often as she used to, but she continues to act as her mother's support system, staying in touch with the staff, and visiting as often as she is able.

Lisa's and Mary's stories are being repeated all over the developed world, with boomers as the caregivers for their aging parents. The current cohort of aging parents—those living in their own homes as well as those occupying beds in nursing homes and apartments in assisted living communities—are composed of the two generations preceding the baby boomers. Will there be a different picture in 2040, when boomers are the ones in their eighties and nineties? One in five of them will not have adult children to provide the kind of emotional, physical, and logistical support that Lisa and hundreds of thousands of others are doing today.

Intergenerational relationships are something people with children take for granted. This is less often the case for those without children, who may never have gotten close to anyone outside their own age group unless they come from large, tight-knit families.

In order to fully understand what child-free people will need later in life, consider the variety of roles adult children play in their aging parents' lives:

Emotional Support

No matter where parents reside, the adult children and grandchildren are usually the ones who visit, discuss family issues, share pictures, take the parent for an outing, and generally stay in close contact with parents as they age. They do this on a regular basis, in person, on the phone, via video conferencing, and in letters and emails, with the women in the family typically taking the lead.

When an older parent has maintained ties to a strong social network (e.g., friends, a place of worship, a senior center, a health club, a bridge group, etc.), additional support may be available when they need help with transportation, a task, or simply need some companionship. This can ease the burden on the adult children, especially if they do not live close by.

Residential Decisions, Real Estate Transactions, and Help with Moving

Very few childless adults reside in assisted living and continuous care communities today. Why? There were no adult children to convince them to make the move. Here is a typical scenario: The adult child or children become convinced mom and/or dad, typically in their late seventies or eighties, should no longer be driving or navigating the stairs in their multi-story home, and the time has come for them to live in a safer place. The adult children then help them "shop" for a new community—often closer to where they and the grandchildren live. Once the new home has been identified, the adult children assist in the difficult and emotional task of downsizing, which usually involves sorting through a lifetime of accumulated "stuff." Once the cherished possessions and memorabilia have been given to family members, sold, or thrown away, adult children help their aging parents move what remains into the new, smaller space. Following the transition, the adult children often handle the real estate transaction to sell or rent the home in which the parents resided. Evelyn had to do all of these things for her mother:

> For five years, Evelyn had tried to convince her widowed mother, Jean, then eighty-seven, to move out of her multi-story home. Evelyn had been raised in the large, multi-story house near downtown Buffalo, New York, and her mother had been living there for fifty-

six years. Jean was adamant about not moving until one night she became dizzy and disoriented, lost her balance and took a fall in the bathroom. She hit her head on the edge of the sink, passed out for a couple of hours and woke up in a pool of her own blood. She managed to make her way to a phone and call Evelyn, who lived several hours away. Evelyn called for an ambulance to take her mother to the nearest hospital, then quickly dressed and started the three-hour drive to the hospital. When she arrived in Buffalo, she found Jean in the emergency room where she had required nine stitches in her forehead and an elaborate bandage for a badly bruised knee and foot. Fortunately, she had no broken bones.

After the accident, Jean reconsidered her position on staying in her own home. Waking up in pain and alone had scared her, and she didn't want to risk another fall. A week later, Evelyn again talked to Jean about moving to a safer place, closer to the town where Evelyn and her husband lived. This time Jean agreed to look at a few possibilities.

Evelyn began spending her weekends researching and visiting assisted living facilities in her area. When she found two she thought her mother might like, she brought Jean down for a weekend and they visited them both. Jean didn't like either one. She thought they were too institutional feeling and she didn't want to eat in a dining room with "a bunch of old codgers and biddies."

Evelyn kept looking, this time with the help of a senior care manager (SCM) who was more familiar with all the options for senior living in her area. The SCM introduced Evelyn to an alternative she had not been aware of: a spacious, one-level, suburban residence that had been converted into a board and care home. The man and woman who owned and ran it were both licensed practical nurses and they seemed dedicated to their calling. They also had several part-time aides who came in to assist in the cooking, cleaning, and care of the three residents they could accommodate. The house had a homey and comfortable feel. Evelyn met the two current residents, who seemed happy and well cared for. She also contacted their families, who told her they were very impressed with the kindness and attention their older loved ones were receiving. Like Jean, the other residents needed supervision, but otherwise were relatively independent, still mobile, and required no intense care. They were happy to be living in a comfortable home with no responsibilities for cooking, cleaning, or household upkeep of any kind. Everyone had their own bedroom and bath, and could have privacy or companionship, as they chose.

To Evelyn's delight, Jean agreed to "give it a try." Together they spent the next six months getting Jean packed and moved. She was reluctant to get rid of anything, but in the end agreed to give most of her prized possessions to her grandchildren and give the rest to charity. She moved into the board and care home with her own bedroom furniture, sheets, towels, and her many family pictures, which were re-installed on the walls of her new bedroom.

There were a few setbacks in her adjustment to the new life, but after two years, Jean finally agreed to let her daughter and son-in-law sell the old family home—a major milestone. Jean, now in her mid-nineties, is happy and well cared for. She gets frequent visits from Evelyn and her two nearby grandkids, one with a new baby—her first great-grandchild.

Where there are no adult children to push the issue, most older people simply stay where they are and cope as best they can. In fact, even when there are adult children in the picture, many, like Mary in our earlier story, are not able to convince the parent to move to a safer location. For many elders, the challenge of learning to navigate a new home (even a much smaller space), meet new people, give up familiar surroundings, and relinquish their treasured independence seems loathsome, insurmountable, or both.

Investments and Other Financial Decisions

As time goes on, some older adults begin to feel they are gradually losing touch with the ever-changing realities of the outside world. Adult children in the prime of life may have a better grasp of the current economic challenges or financial realities of the day. At eighty-five or ninety, a person's mental faculties are often not all they once were. When an older person is aware of this, they might decide to let a capable and trustworthy adult child take over some or all of the financial decisions—maybe handling the investments and doing the income tax calculations—sometimes in conjunction with a fiduciary or financial advisor.

As with a residential move, some older parents see financial help as "interference." There may be strong denial their behavior has changed, even with clear evidence such as an unfiled tax return or the purchase of a peculiar item. The parent's denial makes monitoring the situation more difficult for the adult child who must find a way to check up on the parent without causing too much conflict.

Legal Representation

Children are most often named first on durable power-of-attorney documents (DPOA) for financial matters and health care decisions. A DPOA allows them to have legal proxy for all decisions in one or both of these domains, meaning their signature is treated as the parent's own. Barring a lack of trust among family members, the child named on the document may be the one considered by the parent as the most competent in that area, the one living the closest, or the one considered the most astute or fair.

Bill Paying and Handling Money

An adult child often takes over money management when a parent requests help or starts displaying diminished cognitive abilities. This kind of decline shows up when a person discovers the parent has not been paying bills on time or has been writing checks to unknown recipients. The adult child then takes over the checking account and begins to shift credit information, redirecting bills and financial statements to himself or another of the adult children. Adam's mother, in her late eighties, was aware of her diminishing capacity to handle her own day-to-day financial affairs and asked him for help:

Adam took over his eighty-nine-year-old mother's finances after she had a debilitating stroke. Even before the stroke she had started to talk about giving up her driver's license and was asking Adam to help her with household tasks on a more frequent basis. When the stroke occurred, she became unable to speak or write for four months. Adam recalls having her legal power of attorney a "Godsend." The POA allowed him to get his name added to all her accounts, manage her income, pay her bills, file her taxes, and wade through the mountain of medical bills and statements that arrived daily. He was also able to arrange for her in-home long-term care and to pay himself and his other siblings for out-of-pocket expenses that occurred in the first few days of her hospitalization. After his mother recovered most of her mobility and some of her speech, Adam continued to manage her finances, and his mother expressed relief and gratitude that she had someone to take over for her.

To a great extent, involvement like Adam's in the life of his mother will also protect her (and the estate) from financial scams by those who prey on older citizens.

Medication Management and Help With the Activities of Daily Living

Managing and monitoring medications, ensuring there is food available, and help with personal hygiene are all areas where assistance is often needed as aging parents progress into their final years. In elder care residential communities, staff provide many of these services, yet the adult children continue to take their parents shopping (or shop for them), accompany them to medical appointments, pick up prescriptions, help them put on a nice outfit for a family visit, etc.

Who will be there to help us with these things as we age? The many responsibilities and activities adult children undertake on behalf of their aging parents provide clues to how we should prepare for a later time—a time when we may not be quite as mentally sharp or as physically able as we are today.

The Social Network

As we age, our social network plays a very big role in our well-being. Parents, no matter their age, may include in their social network their children, their children's friends, the parents of their children's friends, their children's in-laws, their grandchildren, and so on. One can imagine how easily and organically this network grows, even with just one or two kids. Those without children, on the other hand, create their social network by design, often including friends, colleagues, neighbors, church members, and other like-minded people as well as any siblings and those offspring interested in staying close.

During the years when parents are changing diapers, helping with homework, and playing chauffeur, those of us who are child-free are developing outside interests, deepening friendships, building their careers, and sometimes playing a role in developing their communities.

The following diagram illustrates the make-up of a typical older parent's social network. The stronger the tie, the darker and wider the connector:

Network of a Parent

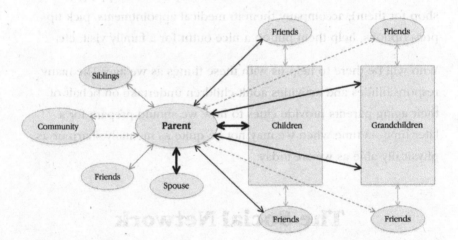

Where does this leave the rest of us? Ties with friends, siblings, nieces and nephews and even community tend to be (and should be) more prominent for us. During the years when parents are changing diapers, helping with homework, and playing chauffeur, those of us who are child-free are developing outside interests, deepening friendships, building careers, and sometimes playing a role in developing communities. Of course, parents also may have strong ties with friends and others who are unrelated, but they are rarely the *primary* connections in their lives.

Isolation and loneliness are the two biggest risks for poor mental health in later life.

The following diagram illustrates a typical social network for an older adult without children. As in the diagram of the older parent, the heavy, bold lines illustrate strong ties; the lighter ones illustrate looser, more tenuous connections.

Network of a Solo Ager

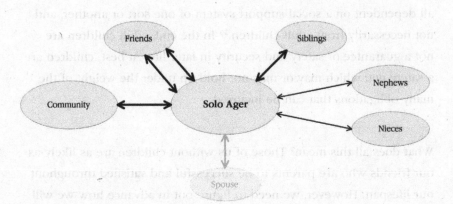

Your own diagram may differ from this one. Everyone has a unique network because no two families are exactly the same, nor are any two individuals.

Research studies over the past twenty years tell us that older adults without children are no different in psychological well-being than those with children.[8]

Child-free adults have found ways to develop healthy social networks as well as methods for coping with difficult situations and solving thorny later-life problems. This healthy psychological make-up bodes well for our ability to cope with the challenges of being older ... if we plan well. These studies also find adults without children are no less satisfied with their lives than older parents.

Isolation and loneliness are the two biggest risks for poor mental health in later life, but again, older parents can be as isolated and lonely as those without children.[9] In fact, some parents reported greater loneliness than those who are childless when their expectations of their adult children went unfulfilled.

Life satisfaction, well-being, and good mental health in later life are all dependent on a social support system of one sort or another, and not necessarily from adult children.[10] In the end, adult children are not a guarantee of safety and security in later life. At best, children are a safety net, which may or may not hold up under the weight of the many obligations that can be incurred.

What does all this mean? Those of us without children are as likely as our friends who are parents to be successful and satisfied throughout our lifespan. However, we need to figure out in advance how we will manage the challenges of aging and whom we can engage to help us.

8   Ingrid A. Connidis, Family Ties and Aging (Thousand Oaks, CA: Sage Publications, 2001).

9   Ibid.

10   Myers, "The funds, friends, and faith of happy people," American Psychologist 55 (2000): 56-67.

The remainder of this book focuses on being proactive about planning—for where we will live, how we will manage our money, who will represent us when we can no longer speak for ourselves, and where we might turn for companionship in the future. Solving those riddles will be the key to our safety, security, and well-being in the latter decades of our lives.

PART II

Enjoying the Second Half of Life

CHAPTER 4.
HAPPINESS AND SATISFACTION

"Grow old along with me! The best is yet to be."

—Robert Browning

Adopting a positive attitude toward our own aging, and aging in general, is a key ingredient in happiness and satisfaction in our later years. This positive attitude requires us to see the "retirement" landscape as a blank canvas on which opportunities abound—for personal development, learning, travel, putting ourselves on the market as a "wise elder" (consultant), getting fit and healthy, volunteering for a cause we believe in, and so much more. Without children and grandchildren, you may have more opportunities (and time) for these explorations than your friends who are older parents. Maintaining a positive attitude will also help in the planning.

Planning is difficult, if not impossible, if we dread our future. If we see aging as a time of new horizons and prepare ourselves for the inevitable challenges, we will be in much better shape to face the future. The older we get, the more dramatically our lack of planning in our earlier days shows up. How young and invincible we were! Luckily, planning for our future is always possible. Unless you are reading this book at one hundred (or more) years of age, you still have time to plan—for the next year, the next decade, or the next half of your life. Estate planning, financial planning, and care planning are the big three in the legal arena, but your planning should not end there. You also need to do some planning for your social and community involvement.

Whether you are still pursuing your career dreams, making money part-time, or living in full retirement from the paycheck world, pursuing something that gives your life meaning and purpose is important for everyone. Does it mean you have to fill a fifty-hour week with philanthropy work or volunteer at five different charities? For some, the answer may be a resounding "yes," but if you cringe at the thought of doing this much "work," there are endless other possibilities for you to consider, whether you say goodbye to your midlife career at fifty, seventy, or even later.

Our social network is an area of life begging for a better strategy. Planning may seem counter-intuitive in this context, but knowing something about who will be part of our future is critical. In the first half of life we form friendships and connections to people we encounter, people whose values and interests align with ours, people who are engaged with life in a way we want to emulate, and people who appear to enjoy our company and have a similar desire to get closer. When we get closer, we call them "friends." These people are then in our "inner circle." Some people have lots of relationships; others select and nurture only a few. At some point, we might transform a relationship into a lifelong partnership or marriage. Also, in our inner circle are family members. For those without children, the inner circle usually includes parents and siblings, and later may include nieces, nephews, and cousins. Most people look at relationships as chance occurrences or serendipity, but I believe we should be more proactive, especially as we get older.

Whether or not you find happiness and satisfaction in the second half of life will depend on how you handle a number of criteria. In my work with people over fifty, I have found there are six important elements to a fulfilling life in later decades:

1. Financial security

2. Commitment to good health and physical well-being

3. Self-awareness

4. Adaptability and flexibility

5. A strong social network

6. Religion, spirituality, or a belief system larger than yourself

I used to include "fun" on the list, but I realized that when my clients could claim they were in possession of all or most of this list, fun naturally followed.

For those who are child-free, some of these six will be *more* challenging, and some will be *less* challenging. In the next few chapters, I expand on each of these, in terms of how they relate to those of us without adult children.

CHAPTER 5. FINANCIAL SECURITY

*"A big part of financial freedom is having your heart and mind free
from worry about the 'what-ifs' of life."*

—Suze Orman

Financial advisors and financial planners are my partners in helping
people plan for a sensible and satisfying life after retirement.
I recommend you seek out one of these professionals to help you
analyze your current financial position. They will use sophisticated
software tools to help you determine where you stand today and what
you must do to have a secure financial future. Online calculators are
also available for those who want to attempt the analysis on their own,
but for most people, working with a professional yields much more
reliable results.

Whether you work with a professional or do it yourself, sound planning
requires answers to the following questions:

- What is your net worth?

- What is your current rate of consumption? (What are you
  currently spending?)

- How much have you saved and what is the rate of return on
  those investments?

- What are your current sources of income?

- What income streams, including Social Security, will be available
  to you in retirement?

- If you are still working, how much longer do you plan to do so?

- If you haven't started Social Security, when should you start taking benefits?

- Based on your health and family history, what is your life expectancy?

The answers to these questions are rarely straightforward. Reliable data about when you can safely quit working and rely on your savings and Social Security to fund your lifestyle requires a complicated formula and a bit of educated guesswork. Many variables must be factored in to determine the point at which your nest egg will be sufficient to provide what you need for the rest of your life. Even though you may plan to work into your sixties, seventies, or even eighties, things can happen. Life can change in a moment, and you want to be as prepared as possible. Because sorting out these twists and turns is challenging, I favor working with a financial advisor or other financial professional.

"Cessation of work is not accompanied by cessation of expenses."

—Cato

There are hundreds of financial advisors and certified financial planners in almost every community in the United States today. Some are private, some are affiliated with banks, and others are with brokerage houses. One way to locate a private financial advisor practicing near you is to go to the Financial Planning Association (FPA) website *(fpanet.org)*. Half of the FPA's website is devoted to consumers. You will find a pull-down menu with guidelines for *finding* a planner near you, *choosing* a planner, and *understanding* the various ways planners charge for their services. You can also use the FPA site to better understand financial planning and how to prepare for a financial planning meeting.

Your local bank may also have a financial planning office. Many of the large nationwide banks have financial services available these days, some with whole offices devoted to retirement planning.

A referral from a friend, relative, or colleague is another excellent way to locate a financial planner. Ask around and get a few names. I encourage you to talk to several financial advisors and decide with whom you feel most comfortable. Finding a financial advisor is much like choosing a physician, a dentist, or a hairdresser. Once you have found some candidates, you may also want to cross-reference your list with your local Better Business Bureau as well as online reviews.

Make sure the person you select has *relevant* experience. Someone who works with clients whose net worth is over five million dollars will not be a good fit for a person who has saved $150,000. A financial advisor with a solid base of clients who are similar in profile to you is a good indicator of relevant experience. Ask how much money is under their management and ask for some examples of clients they are working with (clients can be described without giving away their identity).

Finally, assess the level of comfort and trust you feel in your gut when you are with them. Do they listen to your concerns? Do they disclose their own values and strategy around investing? What experts do they rely on? These are the important criteria for a long-term relationship, or even a few meetings.

If you need to seek low-cost or free advice, most regional FPA chapters perform sporadic pro bono work in partnership with a community service agency or college in their area. You can inquire about those services and special events through the local FPA organization or find a workshop led by a financial advisor through your local community college or adult school.

When you speak with a financial advisor, be sure to mention you don't have children or nearby family. These professionals are seeing more and more people who do not have local support, and they are becoming more adept at recommending good options and safety nets.

A key decision you will have to make, if you haven't already, is when to start collecting Social Security benefits. From the time of its inception until recently, conventional wisdom dictated you should "start taking benefits as early as possible (age sixty-two)." Why? In past years, with a life expectancy of around sixty-eight, the actuaries calculated that the average person would ultimately collect more total dollars by taking benefits early than if they waited until full retirement age or later, even though the monthly payout would have been much larger had they waited.

However, what made sense in 1980 doesn't make as much sense today. Life expectancy has risen sharply and many people can expect to live well into their eighties and beyond, which makes the larger monthly payout a carrot worth the wait. I encourage *healthy* people to wait as long as possible, continuing to earn an income as long as they can, need to, or want to. For every year beyond full retirement age (sixty-six or sixty-seven for baby boomers) your benefits will grow by approximately 8 percent per year until you turn seventy. For many people, the monthly payout at age seventy is almost double what they would have gotten at age sixty-two.

If you are married or divorced, when you are of full retirement age, you may be able to draw a spousal benefit from your current or previous spouse's Social Security account. Depending on your income history, those spousal benefits *might* exceed the money you would collect from your own account, even at age seventy. If so, there is no need to wait beyond full retirement age, because spousal benefits do *not* grow over time. Even if your former spouse has remarried or passed away, if the two of you were married for ten years or more, you are entitled to spousal benefits. Spousal benefits are half of what the spouse collects (or would collect) at full retirement age, regardless of when they filed for their own benefits.

Social Security is complicated and changes have been made to the system in recent years. There are many ways of drawing the benefits to which you are entitled, and I encourage you to talk to a specialist in this area so you can file in the most advantageous way possible. You can do this by making an appointment with a representative in the Social Security office near you or with a financial advisor who has Social Security expertise. For a look at your account, go to the Social Security Administration (SSA) website (ssa.gov). You will discover the amount of money you can expect each month, depending on when you file and start collecting. The SSA website also has a record of every penny you have made, starting with your first paper route or summer internship.

Another element of this equation is how much income you need at this point in your life. Choosing the best time to retire from your midlife profession is not always easy. Many employers will allow you to work part-time, which can be a great first step toward leaving for good. You may also discover you can live on less income than you could as a younger person. Maybe you've paid off your mortgage or maybe you have grown tired of some of the expensive hobbies and "toys" (e.g., motorcycles, ski boats, etc.) you acquired during your younger days. You may also be expecting an inheritance at some point in the next few years. Financial advisors have formulas and calculators to help factor in all of this, and more, to provide you with a solid understanding of your personal financial condition.

You may find you are looking forward to leaving your job of thirty years, but you still need an income. Do you have a hobby you can turn into a business? What might you teach at a trade school or junior college? What side interests might have prepared you for a different kind of job? These pursuits rarely pay what you were making in midlife, but what they pay may be enough to bridge the gap between Social Security and the money you need to maintain your standard of living.

As someone who is child-free, no matter your need for income at this point in your life, the social and community aspects of working may be even more important than the money. Chandra's story illustrates why people often choose to continue working, even when they don't need the income.

When Chandra turned sixty-two, her financial advisor told her she could retire from her job in marketing. Thanks to some solid early investments and a small inheritance from her parents, Chandra could live comfortably on the money in her retirement accounts for the rest of her life. However, as a single, healthy child-free woman, Chandra was aware that occasional lunches with friends and a yearly international vacation were not enough to keep her brain stimulated and provide regular contact with a wide variety of interesting people.

Chandra's employer did not have a part-time position available for her, but they did offer to bring her in on a contract basis. So, Chandra quit her job and returned to the same company on a project-by-project basis at a lower rate of pay than she had been making. Some weeks she went into the office four days, some weeks only one or two.

Initially Chandra rejected the prospect of making an hourly rate that was less than she had been earning on salary. The offer felt like a demotion and a dismissal of her value to the company. Ultimately, though, she realized the new arrangement opened the door for her to have a much more interesting and varied life. When she worked, her time was less regimented. In addition, she often found opportunities to help younger employees or those newer to the job, which was gratifying to her.

Our needs in a job change as we get older. By being willing to let go of her previous ideas about titles and her value to the company, Chandra constructed a very satisfying life for herself in her seventh decade.

Sometimes the pursuit of adventure and a life with maximum satisfaction can end up at odds with the quest for financial security. Janet's story illustrates a life filled with travel and variety, one that might not carry enough certainty for most people, but it offers a glimpse into the choices that must be made at the juncture of life satisfaction and financial security.

Janet was twenty-one when a small US carrier that did international charter flights hired her as a flight attendant. It was her dream job, having grown up in a small, working-class town in Pennsylvania, and she was excited about the life it would offer her. Janet was outgoing, athletic, free-spirited, and wanted to see the world.

She flew for ten years, eventually becoming a senior flight attendant. But visiting the same cities over and over grew tiresome and monotonous for her. During her free time, Janet had learned to hang glide and sail. She became an excellent hang glider pilot, and for several years competed in international competitions with the US Women's National Hang Gliding team. However, sailing was her first love, and when she quit flying she moved to Florida to pursue work as a crew member on large, privately owned sailing vessels.

Janet started her sailing career as an onboard cook, working whenever she could, for both a large charter company in the Bahamas and for private yacht owners. It was hard work, sometimes fun, other times thankless, and after two years she decided she needed to move up the sailing "food chain" and get her captain's license. She enrolled in a two-year program and while continuing to crew, she studied celestial navigation and other nautical skills necessary to take complete command of a large vessel.

In 1989 she completed her studies and her apprenticeship and was awarded her license to captain any vessel under two tons. By then she had forged relationships with most of the sailing community in South Florida, and through this network Janet began to make an adequate living as a charter boat captain.

In 1999, Janet began to feel a little unmoored herself, having never owned a home and spending most of her time somewhere in the Caribbean or en route to the summer ports in the Northeast. She began experimenting around with cooking and eventually started a side business preparing and delivering home-cooked meals. In 2004, Janet left South Florida and headed north, this time to a rural area outside of Chattanooga, Tennessee. She chose a spot on a mountaintop near a hang glider park, and with money she had inherited when her father passed away, built a small home with a guest cottage. At age forty-nine, Janet started her food prep and delivery business as a full-time occupation in a new community. Her new lifestyle also allowed her to move her eighty-five-year-old mother into the adjacent cottage.

The business was successful within two years, and with some interest from large food retailers, Janet figured she would eventually sell the business and use the proceeds to fund her life in retirement. It didn't happen. When the 2008 recession hit, Janet's business was hit hard. All interest from food retailers dried up and Janet decided to call it quits.

For the next five years, Janet worked at a variety of jobs to make a living, and between her mother's Social Security checks and Janet's small income, they did okay. However, none of the jobs Janet held were of lasting interest to her, so she talked to a financial advisor. Together they determined that Janet would be happiest, and do the best financially, back on the water. So in 2013, at age sixty-three, Janet resumed the sailing life, again taking jobs as captain or crew for large deliveries that paid well and allowed her to visit parts of the world she hadn't previously seen. Her mother had passed away the previous year, so Janet had nothing tying her to Chattanooga other than a house she could lock up and leave. In addition, her mother's passing had freed up the guest cottage, and Janet decided to rent it out for additional income. That worked well for her, considering how much she traveled. She also began to rent out the guest bedroom in her home on Airbnb. That added more to her monthly income, and today Janet feels secure that she will be able to enjoy a pleasant lifestyle with several income streams as she ages. Janet never was able to save any of the money she made, but she is still quite strong and healthy at age sixty-six, and looks forward to quite a few more years of sailing.

Janet's and Chandra's stories are very different, but the commonality is that both of them have carved out a life for themselves that is both meaningful and interesting. Janet needs to maximize earnings as best she can at this point, while Chandra will focus on doing what interests her today, regardless of what it pays. They are doing things differently from when they were in their twenties or thirties, and even though Janet doesn't have the financial cushion Chandra can rely on, they each have years of experience to draw upon and, as you will see in many of the following chapters, "security" and a good life is not *all* about money.

NOTE: I am not a financial advisor or financial planner. In this chapter I have provided ideas and opinions about how to organize and stay on top of your financial affairs. I strongly encourage you to seek out professional advice before acting on any of the ideas or suggestions mentioned in the stories or narrative in this chapter.

Chapter 6. Good Health and Physical Well-being

"The greatest wealth is health."

—Virgil

In 1960 the average life expectancy in the United States for a man (at birth) was about sixty-five years. For a woman, life expectancy was seventy-two years. Those statistics sound low to us today, but they were a huge improvement over life expectancy in 1900, which was forty-seven years. Most of the jump during the first half of the twentieth century can be attributed to advances in medicine, which dramatically lowered the rate of infant mortality. Additionally, antibiotics allowed more children to reach adulthood, and better sanitation enabled more women to survive childbirth.

"No drug ... holds as much promise for sustained health as a lifetime program of physical exercise and proper nutrition."

—Dr. Walter Bortz, *Dare to Be 100*

By 2015, life expectancy had jumped to around seventy-seven years for men and over eighty years for women.[11] The more recent jump can also be credited to medical technology, but for a different reason. Today, when someone has a stroke, a heart attack, or gets a cancer diagnosis, their prospects for continuing to live are much greater than they were in 1970. Medical science has found numerous ways to keep us alive,

11   Felicitie C. Bell and Michael Miller, *Life Tables for the United States Social Security Area*, 1900-2100 (Baltimore, MD: Social Security Administration Office of the Chief Actuary, August 2005). Social Security Actuarial Study no. 120. Available at https://www.ssa.gov/oact/NOTES/pdf_studies/study120.pdf.

well beyond the medical event that would have killed us in previous years. According to the Social Security Administration's actuarial tables, the average sixty-five-year-old man, in 2015, had better than even odds of living to age eighty-three and beyond, and the average sixty-five-year-old woman had an even greater chance of living to eighty-five or more.

Most of us want to live into our eighties or nineties—as healthy, functioning human beings. For those of us without children, staying fit and mobile takes on an even more critical notion as we face the challenge of continuing to be independent for as long as possible. We need to keep ourselves as healthy as possible by staying active, keeping our weight at a reasonable level, eating healthfully, and keeping stress levels in check. For some, retirement opens up an opportunity to make healthful changes. Brett made a radical lifestyle change when he left his job:

> Brett worked as a truck driver from age twenty-two until he quit at age sixty-one. He worked for a small company, and in addition to driving the delivery truck, he managed the warehouse, the inventory, and did some of the accounting. By the time he hit sixty, he ached every day and dreaded going to work in the morning. One day he had a falling out with his boss and decided he had had enough. Brett quit the company that day and went home to take stock of his options.

> Brett and his wife, Lynn, are child-free boomers. Lynn had built her own business, which was thriving, producing enough income for them to live comfortably. They decided Brett's working days were over and he became a self-described "house-husband." They let their housekeeper go, and Brett took on all of the home chores. To Lynn's delight, he also developed an interest in cooking and started to experiment in the kitchen. Their dinners, which had been mostly take-out, were now inventive and (usually) excellent.

After six months of cooking, cleaning, and running errands, Brett started to put on weight and realized he needed to burn more calories and get into better cardiovascular shape. During his last physical, while he was still working, his doctor had put him on blood pressure medicine and told him to buy a blood pressure cuff and take a daily reading. After he quit work, Brett tried doing without the blood pressure meds, but found his blood pressure only remained under control with the meds. So, Brett joined a gym and experimented with all the machines and classes offered. Through a couple of personal training sessions, he discovered he also needed to work on his flexibility and balance and keep his upper body strong. The gym had a pool suitable for laps and Brett started to work out in the pool daily. He also sampled the classes and found both yoga and Pilates provided him with the opportunity to work on muscle strength, flexibility, and balance. The classes coupled with the swimming provided Brett with the perfect package for regaining the fitness he had lost over the years of hard work.

After another six months had gone by, Brett felt like a new person. He had lost fifteen pounds, had more energy, and had made some new friends at the gym—people with whom he now goes out to lunch or coffee. Brett, now sixty-three, enjoys his new life tremendously. He loves being the house-husband, spends about two hours a day at the gym, and has a whole new set of friends to hang out with while his wife spends her day at work. As a bonus, when he saw his doctor for his most recent annual physical, his blood pressure had dipped so low his doctor recommended discontinuing the meds.

As Brett's story illustrates, it's never too late to start. Fortunately, we can still correct some bad habits, lose weight, and find an exercise routine to enjoy later in life. I know many people who, during their working years, never managed to find the time to get the exercise they knew they needed. Like Brett, many fifty- and sixty-something men and women discover the joy of hiking or biking or swimming or tennis after leaving their full-time job. Search the Internet and you will find tale after tale of people who lost the extra pounds, lowered their blood pressure and cholesterol, and became much more physically, emotionally, and mentally fit after age fifty. Physical health is not a one-size-fits-all arena—you are the one who must figure out what you need and what works for you.

"To keep the body in good health is a duty, otherwise we shall not be able to keep our mind strong and clear."

—Buddha

Here are some tips to get you started:

- **Get plenty of sleep.** How much is enough? Try to get seven to nine hours a night. If you have trouble *falling* asleep in time to get in a sufficient number of hours, try modifying your food intake in the evening. Spicy foods might be the culprit. Caffeine may be a bad idea any time after noon, and an evening meal heavy on carbohydrates and light on proteins can be helpful. If you have trouble *staying* asleep or wake up several times a night, your mattress may be past its prime and no longer supporting you. You may need to try different sleep positions or talk to your doctor about adjusting your medications. If you sleep with someone who snores, try earplugs. Studies have shown that people who sleep with someone who doesn't snore (or whom they can't hear) have higher quality sleep and sleep for about an hour more than those who sleep with snorers.

- **Get moving.** Find an exercise routine you like and incorporate it into your lifestyle. By now you know if you start something too aggressively, you won't follow through on a regular basis, so find an activity you can ramp up incrementally. Make a commitment to spend at least thirty minutes a day at an activity that raises your heart rate. Start by walking, gradually increase the distance, and then add hills to make it a good heart workout.

- **Be mindful of your stress level.** Take measures to reduce stress if you find you are frequently anxious or worried about something. Stress reduction classes, books, and workshops are available in every corner of the United States today. Take advantage of classes and group support in your community to fix this issue.

- **Avoid added sugar.** The soft-drink habit can be a major source of problems for older adults. Obesity, type 2 diabetes, kidney stones, and osteoporosis have all been linked to sugar in the diet. Sugar-free or diet drinks are not much better. Kicking the soft-drink habit may allow you to enjoy other foods you have been denying yourself, or to lose some weight.

- **Eat more fiber and drink more water.** This one is easy to adopt and doesn't involve sacrifice. Experts have been telling us for years about the value of dietary fiber. Beans, fruit, vegetables, whole grain breads and cereals, and most nuts are all fiber rich as well as tasty and good for you. Water keeps you hydrated, which keeps your skin moist and aids in kidney function.

- **Go for prevention.** Get a physical every year after sixty. Get a flu shot each fall. Ask your doctor about other vaccines that may be right for you. Older adults are much more susceptible to shingles and pneumonia. Vaccines exist for both of these diseases and most insurance will cover them. Make sure you get the appropriate vaccinations for travel if you like to go to more exotic locales. If you are sexually active and not in a monogamous relationship, get checked for sexually transmitted diseases (STDs) on a regular basis. The rates of STDs in people over fifty have skyrocketed in the last fifteen years.

- **Pay attention to your teeth.** Ignoring your dental health in later life can have disastrous implications. Although you are probably less susceptible to decay at this point in your life, you are more susceptible to gum disease, which can affect your overall dental health. In addition, old fillings and caps break down over time and you may need to have them replaced. See a dentist for a checkup at least once a year.

Leaving or changing your job may be the perfect time to embark on a new way of living. Changing a habit is often easier when your daily routine is in flux. If you are in the process of retiring from your midlife career or cutting back your hours, this may be the ideal time to adopt new and healthier habits, physical, mental, and spiritual.

Ken Druck, in a *NextAvenue.org* essay based on his book, *Courageous Aging*, conceived of seven steps for self-care in later life:[12]

1. **Make the decision to change the way you take care of yourself.** This is a promise to yourself that you will do whatever it takes to become a happier, more fulfilled version of yourself.

2. **Define your end goal**. Get clear about your desired outcome and what it looks like. Write it down.

3. **Make a list of the things/people you need to say "no" to.** Stop over committing to people and things that don't contribute to your well-being and don't make you happy.

4. **Lighten you load, unburden yourself and allow yourself some pleasure**. Delegate tasks to others, talk about your journey and goals, and give yourself permission to be happy.

5. **Listen to yourself.** Take the time to just be. Listen to your inner voices. Quiet the negative voices, yours or others'.

6. **Find or create self-care opportunities in all your relationships**. Manage your relationships; don't let them manage you.

7. **Pat yourself on the back for a job well done.** Take note of small changes and triumphs while allowing for new ideas and modifications of your plan.

---

12   "Take the Time to Better Care for Yourself: 7 Steps to the Self-Care You Need," NextAvenue website, http://www.nextavenue.org/take-better-care-yourself/.

Approach your quest for optimum health as a change to your entire ecosystem. Dr. Hendrieka Fitzpatrick, medical director of the Integrated Health Medical Center in Santa Fe, New Mexico adopted the term "ecosystem" to replace the expression mind-body connection. Dr. Fitzpatrick says "in any sustainable ecosystem, there is absolute dynamic interaction at every level. Thus, mind, body, and spirit are all reflections of our internal ecosystem, which is ... a single inseparable entity."[13]

What does that mean? It means you will have the greatest level of success in attaining optimum health if you are in touch with how your thoughts and belief system coincide with your physical health. There are many ways of approaching this. Yoga is a good example of a well-integrated exercise system. As any practitioner of yoga knows, in addition to stretching and toning muscles, yoga involves training the breath and the mind—major components of yoga as a discipline. Taught and practiced in the traditional manner, yoga is as much a meditation practice as a physical activity. Many people find a yoga session clears their mind, leaving them calmer and less stressed.

Many other physical disciplines also incorporate a spiritual and emotional component. In fact, just about any physical routine can be crafted to address the entire ecosystem; yoga and some others (e.g., tai chi) simply have it built in.

For those without children or other close family around a fitness routine or practice can have the added benefit of helping build a support network. The seeds of many strong friendships have been sown in a Jazzercise class, a walking group, a fitness club, on the tennis court, or on the golf links.

---

13   Hendrieka Fitzpatrick, "Move over Barbie and Ken," in *Audacious Aging*, ed. Stephanie Marohn (Santa Rosa, CA: Elite Books, 2009), 129-136.

CHAPTER 7. SELF-AWARENESS, MEANING, AND PURPOSE

"Aging is not lost youth, but a new stage of opportunity and strength."

—Betty Friedan

Who are you? If you are like most people, your answer to that question—at least since you landed your first job—has been "I'm a business owner" or "I sell insurance" or "I teach fourth grade." In other words, you have described yourself by what you DO. Unlike your older parent counterparts, you never thought of yourself as "Brian's mom," or "Kimberly's dad," so you have the advantage of not going through the trauma of the empty nest, but you will still need to re-orient the way you think about yourself after you leave your midlife career and embark on other adventures.

Why am I here?

What is my life about?

What do I want to do with my time, money, and talents?

How can I make a difference in my community and in the world?

Opportunities abound today to explore self-awareness, to define the "new you," and to figure out what makes you happy and adds meaning to your life. Self-development workshops are available through private organizations as well as community colleges and public programs. Transition and life coaches have hung out their shingles in every corner of America, from the smallest towns to the largest urban areas.

Some coaches take on clients through public institutions, like junior colleges and county recreation departments, as well as the private sector.

You can explore your new identity on your own through reading, though the quest can be much harder without someone to provide push-back when you are berating yourself or going off on a quick-fix tangent. That being said, if you choose to pursue it independently, there are more self-help books out there than there are pills in a Costco Tylenol bottle! Choose one oriented toward people in later life. You will find some excellent ones in the reference section of this book.

Starting down any of those paths will lead you on a journey of discovery that will have you confronting questions like:

- How would you describe your personality?

- What are you good at?

- What do you enjoy doing?

- What attracts you?

- What repels you?

- What makes you happy?

- What gets you excited?

- What do you care deeply about?

- What is your life purpose?

- What legacy would you like to leave behind?

No matter which route to self-discovery you choose, the discovery process will change you forever—even if you don't feel the change right away.

A *values clarification* exercise can be an excellent way to begin the journey of self-discovery. The following three Values Clarification

Worksheets will help you approach the process of analyzing what will be right for you—now or in the future:

Values Clarification Worksheet 1

Your values represent what is most important to you in life—what you want to live by and live for. They are the silent forces behind many of your actions and decisions. The goal of this exercise is to become conscious of your values today. Armed with that knowledge, you can explore opportunities or activities for your post-career years. You can be more self-directed and effective when you know which values are most important to you—which ones take priority over others.

> **First, place an "X" by each value that has meaning for you;
> then rank order your top five.**

___ Being with people	___ Having peace and quiet
___ Being loved	___ Having financial security
___ Having companionship	___ Accumulating wealth
___ Loving someone	___ Being physically safe
___ Taking care of others	___ Being comfortable
___ Having a close family	___ Avoiding boredom
___ Having good friends	___ Having fun
___ Being liked	___ Enjoying nature and being outdoors
___ Being appreciated	
___ Being admired	___ Looking good
___ Being independent	___ Being physically fit
___ Having things in control	___ Being healthy
___ Being well-organized	___ Being creative
___ Being competent	___ Growing as a person
___ Being productively busy	___ Living fully
___ Making a contribution to the world	___ Making money
	___ Having a purpose
___ Fighting injustice	___ Seeking greater knowledge
___ Living ethically	___ Being happy
___ Being a spiritual person	___ Being loyal
___ Having a relationship with God	___ Exploring the world

82

Values Clarification Worksheet 2

What do your values say about you as a person?

In what ways have you aligned your midlife career to these values? In what ways has your career *not* been aligned with these values?

What work or other activities have you gravitated to?

What opportunities (jobs, teams, projects) have you said "yes" to?

What work or other opportunities have you said "no" to?

What work activities have felt *un*-aligned with your values?

Values Clarification Worksheet 3

What kinds of leisure activities would align with your values
and give you pleasure?

What kinds of volunteer activities would align with your
values and your skill set?

What kinds of income-producing activities would align with your values and be fulfilling?

What kinds of civic engagement activities would align with your values and your talents?

Once you have a good handle on what matters to you at this stage of your life, you are in an excellent position to find new things to do— pursuits that feed your soul as well as your pocketbook. In this area, there are no boundaries other than those you set for yourself.

Everyone needs a reason to get up in the morning and be glad they're alive. During the early years of our lives, being a child, then being a student, and then having a job—or a series of them—were the major occupations giving those of us without children meaning and purpose. Once you leave the old identity behind, you will need a replacement. Finding this new identity is, for many people, one of the most challenging tasks of venturing into the later stages of middle age and the "retirement" years.

Finding a new purpose resembles the career explorations you may have pursued as a young person. You will start by looking at who you are today and what beckons to you at this point in your life. Those areas of intrigue may be the same things you were interested in as a young adult, or you may find your interests have evolved and are very different than they were forty or fifty years ago. Sally and Dan's stories are both good examples of people who have come full circle with their interests.

As a child, Sally loved everything connected to dance and movement. She took ballet lessons and modern dance. In high school she joined the cheerleading squad and learned to twirl a baton so she could be a majorette. She finished college with a degree in special education and soon discovered teaching took up too much of her time and energy to pursue anything other than aerobic exercise classes at the local YMCA.

Sally enjoyed a thirty-five-year career in education, eventually becoming superintendent of a small school district in suburban Illinois. However, when Sally retired from teaching a few years ago at age sixty-four, she was still physically fit, so she decided to revisit her passion for dance. First, she found an adult school of dance in her area. She enrolled in classes to immerse herself in movement again. Then she started doing some teaching. She now teaches dance basics in a private elementary school and leads classes in movement and flexibility at a local senior center. She even occasionally performs with a local adult dance troupe. Sally believes dance will keep her in good shape well into her later years, and the teaching and performing give her life meaning and purpose.

Dan knew he wanted to be an engineer as far back as he could remember. At age six he was already taking apart his father's bedside alarm clock and putting it back together again. He went directly from college into a career in aerospace engineering, never thinking twice about what he wanted to do with his life—until age fifty-eight when he took an "early-out" retirement package from his employer of thirty-seven years.

As he took stock of his life, Dan realized he had moved well beyond engineering in the last ten years of his employment and would now more truthfully be able to describe himself as a "professional manager" rather than an engineer. Instead of bemoaning his out-of-date engineering skills, Dan got involved with a local scouting organization teaching leadership skills and taking local troops on expeditions into the California wilderness areas, a skill he had learned through childhood backpacking trips with his father.

Both of those examples include a teaching component. Indeed, many people find the best use of the knowledge and skills they have accumulated over their lifetime involves teaching others what they have learned. However, there are also many opportunities that don't involve teaching. More people over fifty than ever before are launching new businesses. In fact, the over-fifty segment of the small business community represents the largest and most successful group of entrepreneurs in the United States.[14] With decades of experience and more time and resources to invest, no wonder older entrepreneurs produce a better showing for their efforts. With the freedom of not having children, you have an even greater advantage: while older parents are spending time and money getting kids launched, you can focus on your own future. Plus, if you are limited in mobility or live in a remote location, today's technologies make home-based businesses more viable than ever before.

"When individuals are living purposefully, they often describe being in flow, experiencing synchronicity, having events and outcomes fall into place. They describe feeling more energy, enthusiasm and satisfaction. And because they're in sync with what they're doing, they are more successful at it."

—*Live Smart After 50* (multiple authors)

The opportunities for reinventing yourself after you leave your midlife career are endless. You can follow a path others have trodden successfully (e.g., buying a franchise) or you can make up your own. What you choose to do will depend on your level of ability and mobility as you age, but there are few reasons for anyone to be idle in their fifties, sixties, seventies, or even eighties if they want to be active and vital.

---

14   "Infographic: Kauffman Index of Entrepreneurial Activity, 1996-2012," Ewing Marion Kauffman Foundation website, last modified April 17, 2013, http://www.kauffman.org/multimedia/infographics/2013/kiea-1996-2012-infographic. This webpage further notes: "Up-to-date information is available at www.kauffmanindex.org."

At age sixty-five, if you are still healthy, your life expectancy will be in the mid-eighties, and many people are now living active lives into their late eighties and nineties. Even with plenty of money, would you really want to sit around and do nothing for twenty-five or thirty years?

Do you need to continue to make a living, and if so, for how long? You will need to answer that question before deciding what kind of pursuit fits you best (e.g., should you become a master gardener for *fun*, or should you start a mail-order plant sale business?). Your financial advisor can help you answer that question.

Many people get to this stage of life and think they either have to stay in their current job/career or quit working entirely. For many people the right answer lies somewhere in the middle. That doesn't mean you *shouldn't* stay at your current job beyond the typical retirement age; you just may not *have* to.

If you are lucky, your employer may be among the small minority of organizations offering *phased retirement*, an option that would enable you to continue working, but at a reduced level—say, three days a week or two weeks on and one week off. Some employers include the opportunity to telecommute (work from home) several days a week as part of their phased retirement program. Other employers have included sabbaticals, in which soon-to-retire individuals can take several months off to try out a retirement occupation or location. One retail company lets its older employees transfer to a Sunbelt location for part of the year. That arrangement helps the employee and the employer, since many retailers need to staff up for the winter months in states like Florida and Arizona.

As someone without children, these suggestions may be appealing to you. When you don't have to worry about being near the grandkids, the whole world opens up with opportunities. This is your time to experiment—with a life, and with a livelihood. We will further explore opportunities for making an income in Chapter 11.

Consider Your Legacy

Another way of looking at what is important to you at this stage of your life is to think about your *legacy*. Just because you don't have children doesn't mean you can't leave something behind that will make the world a better place. Legacies aren't necessarily tangible or monetary. Meg Newhouse, in her wonderful book, *Legacies of the Heart*, describes it this way:

"A legacy is anything—tangible or intangible, of any size. Our legacies are what we intentionally or unintentionally give, bequeath, or leave behind during our life or at our death that will last beyond our death. Some of us leave public legacies in the form of organizations and their work, published or sold artistic works, public buildings and other structures, or widely disseminated ideas. But most of our legacies remain in the private realm of family, friends, colleagues, students, and other individuals whose lives we have significantly influenced. Legacies are the imprint of our lives that endures in some form."

My friend Sondra (she is no longer living, so I am using her real name) was both a mentor and a friend to me. Twelve years my senior, she was further along in a career field I was just entering. I met her when I was twenty-eight, not as a colleague or coworker, but as the girlfriend of a man my first husband brought home to dinner one evening.

At the time we lived in Colorado Springs, and the fellow had come to town to visit the company where my husband worked. They stayed late into the evening, and as the men talked business, Sondra and I got to know one another. She lived in western Kentucky where she was born and raised, but was on the verge of moving to Phoenix to take a job with a consulting firm headquartered there. She had recently received her doctorate in education from Vanderbilt University, for which she had commuted to class two hours each direction, two days a week for four years. The dedication and perseverance she demonstrated in finishing that program impressed me.

At the point I met her, Sondra had just started to build a career in organizational development (OD). I didn't yet know much about the fairly new OD field, but everything she told me about her work fascinated and intrigued me. I had recently completed my master's degree and was teaching at a junior college in Colorado Springs, but I knew after our discussion that evening that I wanted a career like hers.

Sondra and I stayed in touch for the next eighteen years of our lives, through divorces and remarriages, through jobs and consulting assignments, and through the completion of my PhD. For about a four-year stretch, we had the good fortune of living near one another in Silicon Valley. By then I had found a way to shift my career from teaching to corporate training and eventually into organizational development. Sondra had attained great success as a consultant and traveled frequently, but she always made herself available to shepherd me through the rough spots in my burgeoning consulting work, offering suggestions for handling difficult clients and tricky organizational politics. She helped me understand how to think more broadly and creatively about my clients' issues and offer them alternative solutions—without sounding like I knew how to run their business better than they did.

Sondra developed ovarian cancer at age sixty-two. I wanted to give back in some way for the years she had mentored me and been my spiritual guide, so I spent the last month of her life with her in western Kentucky where, surrounded by her family and a few close friends, she taught us all how to put closure on a life well lived. Sondra left a huge legacy for many people, including her own children. I continue to use and cherish her legacy, and will do so throughout the rest of my life.

"In a kind of positive-feedback loop, a concern with legacy by itself extends our sense of time and space. In pondering our legacies, we naturally think back to our roots and forward even beyond, to the next generation or to the kind of society and planet we want to bequeath ... within our families or friendship circles and our local communities ... the larger picture thus provides a context, compass, or catalyst for our increased desire to give back and leave a positive imprint."

—Meg Newhouse, *Legacies of the Heart*

We leave behind a legacy whether we want to or not. Think about the legacies you have inherited—from your parents, your teachers, and others who have been influential in your life. In many cases, these people may not even have known they were leaving you a legacy, but you got it, nonetheless. Some legacies are negative, some are positive; some are left deliberately, but most are left by default. Many default legacies are genetic. You may have been told you have your father's nose or your mother's gait. You didn't choose those legacies and neither did they.

Without children, we won't be leaving genetic legacies for anyone, so we have an opportunity to sculpt whatever legacy we want to leave. You may have secondary family members you would like to influence—maybe nieces or nephews. You can leave them material things of course, like money, jewelry, or tools, but you also have the opportunity to leave them something less tangible, like your attitude toward life, your problem-solving strategies, your inquisitiveness, your reactions to change, or the value you place on lifelong learning.

When my two nieces were young, I knew they would not inherit from their parents the value I place on education, yet I knew the more education they got, the more choices they would have in their lives. I talked to them about college at every opportunity, sharing with them the ways I have used my graduate education to open doors and find interesting ways to make a living. I also offered to help pay for any educational pursuit they chose after high school.

One niece took me up on the offer, went to a four-year college, got a fine arts degree, and has had a number of interesting jobs in the art world. Today she runs her own successful business teaching classes in basic drawing and painting. The value of education is the legacy I leave her, and I am certain she will pass it along to her two daughters.

You don't have to have done anything deliberate or forceful to leave a legacy. Often the quietest people leave the most enduring legacies.

The following worksheet will give you an opportunity to think more about the legacies you have been left and the legacies you wish to leave.

Leaving a Legacy Worksheet

Legacies you *inherited:*

Describe a legacy someone left for you and the person who left it

Describe what you have done as a result of receiving that legacy?

Describe a second legacy someone left for you and the person who left it

Describe what you have done as a result of receiving that legacy?

Describe a third legacy someone left for you and the person who left it

Describe what you have done as a result of receiving that legacy?

Legacies you want to *create:*

What lessons have you learned that you would like to pass along to others?

What values have you cherished that you would like to pass along to others? Who would you like to see inherit them?

What are some actions you can take or changes you can make that would help you create these legacies?

CHAPTER 8. ADAPTABILITY AND FLEXIBILITY

"The wiser mind mourns less for what age takes away than what it leaves behind."

—William Wordsworth

When we were in our teens and twenties, our whole lives stretched out before us. We were still forming our opinions, our political beliefs, our preferences for one food or another, action movies or comedies, living in the country, the suburbs or the city, and what we might do for a career or job. We were flexible and strongly influenced by pop culture, the media, and (occasionally) our parents, though we were loath to admit the latter. As we settled into midlife, these preferences crystallized—a natural part of maturation. You've probably heard the expression "set in his ways." It's used to describe someone intractable in their opinions or locked into a certain way of doing things, to the exclusion of other alternatives. As we progress into and through middle age, these preferences and biases often become even more solid and impermeable. This transition happens to everyone, but crystallization can backfire as we get older. Ironically, in later life *de*-crystallizing becomes more important. We need to explore our areas of rigidity and determine how those fixed ideas may be limiting our lives or keeping us in situations that have outlived their usefulness.

Lisa provides a good example of how a rigid thought pattern can affect your life.

Lisa is a single woman in her early sixties, a third-generation San Franciscan from a tight-knit family that had emigrated from Italy around 1910. She was surrounded by siblings as well as many cousins, nieces, and nephews. In recent years, the younger generation in her family had started to leave the city because of the high cost of living, most of them moving to somewhat less-expensive towns east of San Francisco.

As Lisa and her contemporaries—friends as well as same-generation family members—started retiring from their midlife careers, Lisa was caught in a difficult situation. The upkeep on her eighty-year-old Victorian house was becoming prohibitive, and the pervasive fog and humidity were problematic for her developing arthritis. Over the course of five years, she watched many of her close friends and family members move to the much-sunnier east bay while she remained in the city, tied to a mindset of being a San Franciscan, a city person. She believed she would feel bored and out-of-place elsewhere.

Do you see a little of yourself in Lisa? What are your areas of rigidity? Sometimes our inflexibility shows up with regard to food. The more we learn about what keeps us healthy—especially in later life—the more our diets need to change and flex with new information. Most baby boomers grew up on "PBJ"—Peter Pan peanut butter with Welch's grape jelly on Wonder Bread. We ate Tater Tots and fish sticks and the occasional TV Dinner. If we were lucky, our parents were at least listening to the conventional wisdom at the time and not letting us eat too many sweets or sugary sodas.

As we grew up, even more "convenience" foods hit the market and we added the more adult versions of the PBJ to our diet—things like BLTs, pizza, burgers, and fries. At about the time we hit our forties, food scientists started to wag their fingers at us, lecturing us about the sugar and fat in those foods and what they were doing to us. Nutrition scientists were discovering which foods would keep us healthy and which ones were more likely to send us to an early grave. Now, as baby boomers become older adults, most of us know what we should and shouldn't eat. But are we changing our habits?

If you are diabetic, are you avoiding sugar and simple carbohydrates? If you have high blood pressure or other heart problems, are you staying away from added salt? Are you curbing your fat intake to keep your cholesterol in check? To stay healthy, we need to adapt our food choices as we get older, changes that will differ from person to person.

How many times have you heard a friend say something like, "I have to keep nagging my mother to take her blood-thinners. I don't want her to end up in the hospital again!" *You* aren't going to have an adult child calling every day to make sure you follow a diet regimen or take your medications. Your spouse might or might not be willing or able to nag you, and if you are single, you will have to keep yourself in line—with discipline and tenacity, plus a willingness to change your routine. The ability to see the world differently and the willingness to adapt to a new reality are critical as we age.

Flexibility permeates many of the other topics in this book: how we see ourselves, what we do with our time, where we live, and more. The following quiz will help you identify how adaptable you are when life throws you a curve.

Change and Adaptability Quiz

Circle the letter that best describes how you would feel or react in the following situations:

1. Your next-door neighbors just put their house on the market. In addition to feeling sad they are leaving, what else do you feel?

    A. Shocked they would abandon the neighborhood and the house they call home

    B. Very concerned the new neighbors might be noisy or careless about their property

    C. A little anxious, but ready to welcome the new people when they move in

    D. Excited about having new people on the block

2. A new colleague was just hired to work on your team. What do you do?

    A. Keep interacting only with the old team members, whose personalities and roles you know

    B. Ignore her until she asks for your guidance or advice

    C. Welcome him cordially and then leave him alone

    D. Welcome her, ask how you can help her feel included, offer to show her around the building, ask her to share lunch

3. The city is doing street repairs, so you need to find a new route for your daily walk. How do you feel? What do you do?

   A. Angry your routine was disrupted. You stop walking until the repairs are finished

   B. Somewhat discombobulated because you don't know where to walk while the repairs are under way. You stop walking for a few days, then reluctantly find a new route

   C. Motivated to find a new route. You immediately do so

   D. Excited you will now get to experience new sights and activities during your walk (of course you didn't walk the same route every day to begin with)

4. A new supermarket with a reputation for excellent produce and competitive prices has just moved into town. You …

   A. Ignore the new market and keep on shopping at the same store where you have always shopped. The old grocery has served your needs just fine, and you believe in loyalty

   B. Go once to check out the new store, but return to your old store because you know where to find everything there

   C. Check out the new store right away to determine which you prefer, now that you have options

   D. Embrace the new store, shopping there exclusively for six months and encouraging all your friends to do the same. You want to make sure the new store succeeds, giving you permanent options

103

5. You are doing an important task with a self-imposed deadline. A friend calls to share some important news and is eager to get your feedback. You ...

> **A.** Ignore the ringing phone, listen to the message, go back to your task
>
> **B.** Ignore the ringing phone, listen to the message, then call your friend to make an appointment to chat later
>
> **C.** Determine the task can wait fifteen minutes, answer the phone, and listen to the friend's news, giving her as much feedback as you can, but cutting the call short to return to the task
>
> **D.** Determine the task can wait, answer the phone, and have a forty-five-minute chat with your friend

6. Your doctor has just given you a diagnosis of high blood pressure and advised you to purchase a blood pressure cuff, measure your blood pressure twice a week, and cut your salt intake to one teaspoon a day. You are most likely to ...

> **A.** Ignore the warning, tell no one, and continue your lifestyle as before
>
> **B.** Think about the advice for a few months, then begin to share the information with a few close friends or spouse and start looking at cuffs in pharmacies
>
> **C.** Purchase the cuff right away, then put it in a nearby drawer for regular use, and begin gradually using less salt
>
> **D.** Purchase the cuff at a pharmacy on the way home from the doctor's office, set it up in the bathroom for regular use; upon arriving home, dump out all salt shakers, and resolve to buy no more heavily processed foods

7. You are waiting at the gate to board your flight to Europe. The gate agent announces they have changed aircraft and everyone will need a new seat assignment. When your turn arrives to talk to the agent about your seat, you ...

   A. Express your distress about the aircraft switch and ask to have your same row and seat

   B. Express your concern that you may not get the aisle seat you had reserved and ask to be given a seat as similar as possible to the one you had originally reserved

   C. Ask the agent what's available on the new plane and select a new seat from the options you are given

   D. Take whatever new seat the agent assigns you, looking forward to meeting your new seatmates

8. A friend offers you last-minute tickets to an event he knows you will enjoy. You had made plans to answer some emails that evening and watch two new TV shows you had recorded. You ...

   A. Thank him and tell him it's too late to change your plans for that evening

   B. Thank him and tell him you will take the tickets only if you are his last resort

   C. Thank him, accept the tickets, and hurry home to at least get the emails done before the show

   D. Thank him and eagerly accept the tickets, then call a companion to accompany you. The heck with the emails; they can wait

9. You arrive with a friend at a restaurant on a Saturday evening, only to discover they have no record of the reservation you made a week ago. Now they have no table for you and the waiting list is already lengthy. You ...

   A. Get upset and show them the evidence on your phone that you called them a week ago

   B. Sigh, take a place on the waiting list, and sit in the bar to await a table

   C. Let your friend decide what to do

   D. Turn to your friend and say, "Now we can try the new place down the block"

10. Your dentist has just retired and sold his practice to a young dentist you have never met. You ...

   A. Are sad and upset he has abandoned you and fearful you will never find another dentist you trust

   B. Are upset you will now have to find a new dentist. You go two years without seeing any dentist at all, then ask for referrals from others

   C. Are somewhat dismayed at this turn of events, but immediately start asking for referrals for someone your friends like and trust

   D. Send a congratulatory note to your old dentist and look forward to finding a new dentist—maybe the one who bought the practice. He's probably fresh out of school and up-to-date on all the latest dental technology

11. You are out with a few friends for dinner. The plan was to have an early dinner, then see a movie at the nearby cinema. However, the evening is warm and beautiful and one friend suggests you abandon the movie idea and go to a nearby park for a walk and to watch the sunset. You respond by ...

   A. Saying no, you prefer to keep the original plan; you are programmed for a movie no matter how spectacular the sunset promises to be

   B. Telling the group you are uncomfortable changing plans at the last minute

   C. Keeping silent and going along with what the rest of the group decides

   D. Saying yes, thinking you can see the movie another time; beautiful evenings are to be cherished

12. Just before leaving for a party, your cat/dog had an "accident" on the shirt you were planning to wear. You ...

   A. Call the party hostess and let her know you won't be able to attend

   B. Spend an hour getting the stain out of the shirt—putting it through a short wash cycle, drying it, and ironing it—and then put the shirt back on, arriving at the party quite late

   C. Toss the shirt into the laundry basket, stain and all, put on a different outfit, and head to the party

   D. Decide you can live without the shirt, toss it in the trash, find another outfit, and head to the party

Scoring:

Give yourself **one** point for every **A** you selected   _____

Give yourself **two** points for every **B** you selected   _____

Give yourself **three** points for every **C** you selected   _____

Give yourself **four** points for every **D** you selected   _____

Total   _____

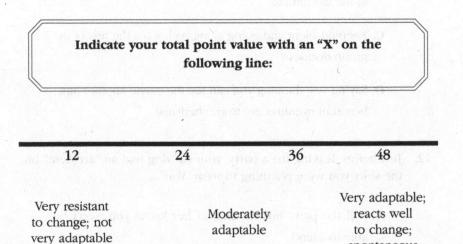

> **Indicate your total point value with an "X" on the following line:**

12	24	36	48
Very resistant to change; not very adaptable	Moderately adaptable		Very adaptable; reacts well to change; spontaneous

How did you score? If you scored lower than thirty, take a look at ways you can practice being more flexible. Now that you are aware of your tendencies, you can be more observant of your flexibility in everyday life. Spontaneity is connected to flexibility and adaptability. If you can coach yourself to be more spontaneous, you will find yourself practicing flexibility in a fun and interesting way.

CHAPTER 9. A STRONG SOCIAL NETWORK

"And in the sweetness of friendship let there be laughter, and sharing of pleasures. For in the dew of little things, the heart finds its morning and is refreshed."

—Kahlil Gibran

Being child-free, we have a more limited network of relationships than our parent peers. As the diagrams in Chapter 3 illustrate, children add complexity to the relationship map. Like a mathematical formula, each child represents another factor in the equation. The children's relationships with their friends and, eventually, in-laws become part of the parents' relationship network as well.

If you are part of a couple, the strongest connection in your social network is probably your partner. If you are single, the strongest connections might be with your siblings or close friends. Lesser, but still important, relationships are with cousins, sometimes nieces and nephews, and often with additional friends. Community ties are often stronger for people without children as well. Of course, these are generalizations. We are all different. Some of us are married; some are not. Some have no siblings; hence, no nieces and nephews. Some in the child-free ranks have siblings who are also child-free. Some have siblings who have predeceased them and left nieces and nephews in their wake.

Strong evidence exists for a direct connection between social support resources (relationships) and good mental health. Strong social networks have buffering effects when we go through painful events or experience temporary stressors. In fact, child-free individuals with a solid social support network are mentally healthier than parents with a modest or weak social network.

"Because everything of value that we will know in this life comes from our relationships with those around us. Because there is nothing material that measures against the intangibles of love and friendship."

—R. A. Salvatore

Use the following worksheet to create a representation of your own social network. Fill in the bubbles with the names of those who matter to you. Draw heavier lines (or use a brighter color) for the closest or most important relationships and thinner lines for the more distant or less important ones. Feel free to add more bubbles if you need them. The more precise you can be with this exercise, the better you will be able to analyze the health of your network.

Personal Relationship Network

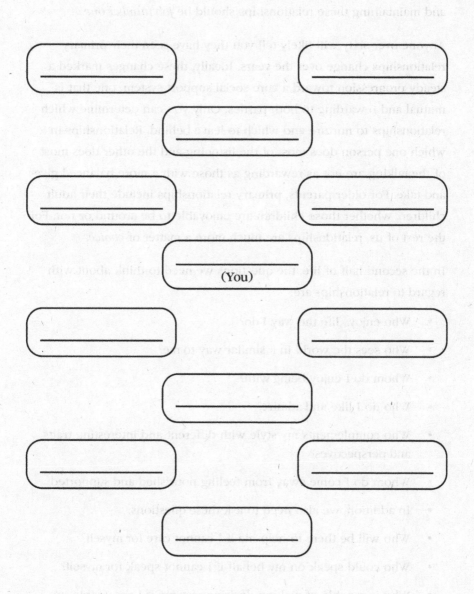

(You)

Relationships are critical for everyone, and especially for those of us who are child-free. Friends, relatives, and community ties are not just nice-to-have pieces of your life; they are key to your survival! Building and maintaining these relationships should be *job number one.*

Anyone over sixty will likely tell you they have seen their primary relationships change over the years. Ideally, these changes marked a steady progression toward a core social support system, one that is mutual and rewarding to both parties. Only you can determine which relationships to nurture and which to leave behind. Relationships in which one person does most of the listening and the other does most of the talking are not as rewarding as those with a more balanced give-and-take. For older parents, primary relationships include their adult children, whether those children are enjoyable to be around or not. For the rest of us, relationships are much more a matter of *choice.*

In the second half of life, the questions we need to think about with regard to relationships are:

- Who enjoys life the way I do?

- Who sees the world in a similar way to me?

- Whom do I enjoy being with?

- Who do I like and admire?

- Who complements my style with different and interesting traits and perspectives?

- Whom do I come away from feeling nourished and supported?

- In addition, we also need to ask these questions:

- Who will be there to help me if I cannot care for myself?

- Who could speak on my behalf if I cannot speak for myself?

- Who is capable of making decisions for me if I am unable to make them for myself?

As you read this chapter, you may be thinking "my friends are people I know from work" or "I've been too busy to maintain most of my friendships; seeing my family and getting my work done is all I can do" or even "I don't have time for socializing and friends; I'm always too busy with (fill in the blank)." This is a scary way to enter your later years. We all need people who know and care about us, regardless of our family situations. Even if you have a spouse or life partner, you need more than two or three other people around you to fill in the picture.

I'm not suggesting an army of people. Five to ten good friends or close relatives are the right number. Remember, people may not stay in your life forever, so we have to guard against relying on one or two people exclusively, and that includes spouses. People leave our lives for lots of reasons. They move away, they become ill, their interests or priorities change, and—increasingly as we get older—they die. The reality can be harsh. With friends, safety is found in numbers. Like the royal families of England, always demanding their queens produce "an heir and a spare," we need spare companions in a variety of ages in our lives.

George Vaillant, one of the fathers of modern gerontology, was a professor and psychiatrist at Harvard Medical School during the middle of the twentieth century. In 1938, he began what turned out to be one of the longest-running studies of aging in the world. His original objective was to determine what constituted a happy and successful life. Starting with the advantage of a Harvard education, the (all male) subjects were expected to excel at most of the criteria in the study, with a strong correlation to their success in school itself. In fact, what he found was that *relationships* were what mattered most in achieving both happiness and success.

Vaillant continued to track these men long after the study was published, following a sizeable number of them into their *nineties*. Through surveys and interviews, he tracked their physical and emotional health as they aged. He concluded "relationships are the key to healthy aging." He advocated cultivating younger friends for their energy and fresh perspective: "You must have somebody outside yourself to be interested in—not just hobbies or crossword puzzles or your stock account—but flesh and blood." He went on to assert: "In the same way you exercise, pay your taxes, and eat a healthy diet, you need to start replacing friends as soon as you lose them, particularly around retirement age."[15]

If you are finding you need to bolster your friendship network and you aren't sure where to start, you may find the following suggestions helpful:

- Look around you. Who lives in your neighborhood that you don't yet know? Could you form a stronger friendship with a close neighbor?

- What are you interested in? Join one of the thousands of "Meetups" occurring in communities every day around the United States (meetup.com). The meetup.com website is an organizing mechanism. Based on your geographic location, you may find a small handful or, in larger metropolitan areas, dozens of groups of people sharing your interests who meet face-to-face on a regular basis. Stitch (stitch.net) also links people who share interests. Stitch operates more like a dating site, where you can browse a database of members to find someone to chat with and maybe meet—for companionship or romance. Stitch was designed to end loneliness for older single adults. A distinguishing feature of Stitch is their travel component. When I checked out the trips being planned for 2017/2018, the list included Cuba, Yosemite National Park, a cruise from London to Stockholm, Alaska, Peru, Florence, Italy, New England and Nova Scotia, Lake Tahoe, Easter Island, and more.

---

15   Excerpted from Elizabeth Pope, "A Longer Life is Lived with Company," *NY Times,* September 11, 2012. Available at http://www.nytimes.com/2012/09/12/business/retirementspecial/for-older-adults-close-connections-are-key-to-healthy-aging.html.

- Meetup.com and stitch.net are examples of the many Internet sites whose mission is to bring people together. These two are well entrenched and have a good track record of success.

- What do you care about? Whether your passion is local politics, animal rights, road safety, or practicing medicine halfway around the globe, volunteer opportunities exist for you to help change the world and at the same time meet like-minded people. If you are unsure about how to get started, try the website volunteermatch.org. Based on your zip code and the interests you specify, the website will feed you a list of activities taking place in your area over the next few weeks.

- Take up a sport you enjoy (or used to enjoy twenty years ago). Once again, the Internet can be a great ally for finding the right group or a like-minded partner. Explore meetup.com as a resource for like-minded sporting companions.

- Go back to school. Is there a language you have always wanted to learn? A hobby you would like to pursue? A computer skill you wish you possessed? These courses are available at your local junior college or university extension. Classes are a great place to meet new friends with similar interests. In addition to extension programs at local colleges, Osher Lifelong Learning Institute (OLLI) programs can be found on the campuses of many colleges across the country. They operate a series of programs designed for "seasoned adults" (fifty or older). A typical roster of local OLLI courses includes both short (two-to-three hour) and long (multi-day) courses. Through OLLI, you can study a language, a country, a historical period, a culture, learn how your brain works, study a musical genre, attend a symphony, be an armchair traveler, and much, much more. To find the OLLI program center nearest you, check out the Bernard Osher Foundation website (osherfoundation.org).

- Are you interested in traveling? Taking a trip with like-minded other adults can spark some terrific friendships. Road Scholar (formerly Elder Hostel) is a tour company that serves only older adults. Many people who are child-free and single, or whose spouses choose not to accompany them, travel alone and Road Scholar can pair you with a roommate that shares your interests or provide you with a single room during your trip. You may also want to explore the adventures that Overseas Adventure Travel (OAT) offers. They are somewhat more expensive than Road Scholar, but still reasonable, and frequently waive the "single supplement" fee, so you can have your own room without paying extra.

- Start online. In the same way young people are now meeting and getting to know one another through social media before they ever have a face-to-face encounter, older people can begin to form friendships in the same way. You can connect with all kinds of special interest groups by searching online. If you enjoy knitting, enter the word "knitting" or "I like knitting" into a search engine and see what comes up. When I entered "knitting" into my browser, an interesting and friendly-looking site called "ravelry. com" came up on the first page. I clicked on the link and found a site for knitters and crocheters to share patterns and ideas with one another. I'm not a knitter, so I didn't join, but the site looked simple and enticing.

If you find you are out of practice in the art of developing and nurturing new relationships, remember, every relationship begins somewhere, so assume you will need to take the first step. Once you have identified a person you would like to know better, take the first step by asking her/him to join you for coffee, lunch, a walk, or a game of golf or tennis.

"To have a friend, you have to be a friend."

—Lillian Geber

Once you are engaged in an activity, get to know one another by asking questions to help you become more familiar with each other's lives. Try to balance the conversation by doing as much asking as telling. If you find you are performing a monologue, you are not asking enough questions. Back off and start fresh. Try questions like, "Did you see the movie about ...? What did you think of it?" "How long have you lived in the neighborhood? What led you to settle here?" "How do you spend your time?" "Do you have hobbies you enjoy?" Focus on non-inflammatory topics, something neutral in nature. There will be plenty of time for you to learn about each other's political and religious persuasions later.

My husband likes to quote something his mother told him when he was in junior high: "To *have* a friend, you need to *be* a friend." Somewhere along the way, as your relationship develops, look for an opportunity to do something for your new friend. Offer a ride to the airport or an invitation to a dinner party. You may have the opportunity to offer caregiving after a minor medical procedure. These kinds of small gestures are the glue that holds relationships together.

"Building community" gives us another way of looking at the relationship component of being child-free. Since we don't have the default community that comes along with having kids, we need to create our own. Your community might include blood relatives: siblings, nieces, nephews, grand-nieces/-nephews, cousins, etc. It might also include close friends who embody the potential for a lifelong relationship. You are the one who must determine who belongs in your community, so consider embracing family *and* friends in your inner circle.

What about stepchildren? There isn't an ironclad answer. Only you know the quality and intensity of your relationship with them. The level of intimacy you have with them often depends on when you entered each other's lives. Did you play a major role in raising your stepchildren? Do they live nearby? Do they share your values? Are you close to them? Do they confide in you? If you are leaning toward including them in your plans for aging, you should have a conversation

117

with them. They will be as puzzled as you are about how to relate to you if their blood parent predeceases you.

The following worksheets can help in evaluating your current relationships. They give you a chance to dig deep and analyze which relationships are healthy and which are not, which are worth pursuing for greater depth, and which can be laid to rest. The worksheets will also challenge you to take a look at how your relationships have changed over the years.

Relationship Evaluation Worksheet

You can use the Relationship Status Guidelines and the Relationship Evaluation Worksheet to evaluate the important relationships in your life today. Use the first column to list all the important people in your life. Be sure to list all siblings, nieces, nephews, parents, and in-laws (if applicable), regardless of how often you see them. In addition, list friends, colleagues, and more distant relations (aunts, uncles, cousins, etc.). Once you have listed your key relationships, use the Relationship Status Guidelines to complete the third and fourth columns.

	Relationship Status Guidelines
Excellent	This person knows me well and we have mutual trust and respect for one another. We see each other frequently and have meaningful and genuine interaction. I feel emotionally enriched after spending time with this person. I definitely want to maintain this relationship.
Good	This person knows me pretty well. We may not see each other as much as we would like, but we talk on the phone or exchange email regularly. I see the potential for this relationship to be closer, but I would need to make some changes (more frequent efforts at communication, travel, a move by one party).
So-so	I seldom see this person because of geographical distance. OR this person presents challenges to me because of their values, lifestyle, political views, or other issues where they differ from me. OR this is someone with whom I have a strained relationship because of past differences. OR there are other reasons I put them in this category.
Poor	This is someone I find stressful to be around. My relationship with this person is quite strained. OR I simply never see them. I have had a painful incident in the past. OR we often get into an argument when we see one another. I consider this person to be "difficult" to be around and I often actively avoid her/him. This is someone who leaves me exhausted when we spend time together.

Relationship Evaluation Worksheet			
Name	Relationship	Excellent, Good, So-so or Poor?	Change Needed?

Thinking about Relationships NOW

How have your key relationships changed over your adult life?

How has your role in those relationships changed?

What are you noticing now about your relationships? Are they different from when you were in your twenties? Forties?

What can you do to deepen the relationships you want to keep?

What can you do to breathe new life into key relationships
that have gone dormant or have experienced tension or strife?

Think of your social network as your *family of choice*. Your network
should consist of people you want around you—in good times and
in bad. Most of the members of your network should be friends and
family you would not hesitate to call at three o'clock in the morning if
you need help or consolation. Ask yourself now, "Are these the people
with whom I'm willing to share the final days of my life?"

CHAPTER 10. A BELIEF SYSTEM LARGER THAN YOURSELF

"Spirituality, as expounded by the great saints and sages of the past, is a very broad path. It accommodates all types of belief systems. You need to satisfy everyone."

—Mata Amrtanandamayi Devi, Hindu spiritual leader

Most studies on aging contain a reference to the importance of a belief system in later life. The question, "Is there something wiser or bigger than myself I can count on for guidance and comfort?" becomes critical to the vast majority of elders in almost every society. A deepening sense of faith in an unknown and unknowable *something* seems to offer solace for the walk through the unfamiliar and sometimes frightening landscape that greets us as we age, though a deepening faith may have arisen earlier for those who experienced the loss of a family member or loved one earlier in life.

Returning to a religious or spiritual practice happens naturally for some, as they feel drawn to the habits and rituals learned in childhood, whether or not they discarded those beliefs and practices as an adolescent or young adult. Others, seeking to find a spiritual connection at this stage of life, may choose to embrace an entirely new practice.

For some, traditional religion represents a sanctuary for the spirit, an enduring faith, passed down from parents and grandparents. For others, the concept of religion has become something of a lightning rod; it evokes images of extremism, narrow-mindedness, even violence. However, there is little doubt a spiritual practice of some sort helps us make the shift from a life of externally defined success to one of significance and purpose—which for most of us, is the ultimate desire as we age.

Despite disparate meanings and perceptions, spirituality in the context of aging cannot be ignored. Throughout recorded history, there are testaments to the power of faith at the end of life. Expressions like "there are no atheists in the foxholes of war," or "as her body failed, she grew closer to God," are common in literature. References to a growing spirituality as we age pepper the research on death and dying. Is spirituality merely a salve for the fear of dying? Or is there something more to it? You'll have to answer that for yourself.

Our siblings and friends who raised kids may have kept a religious attachment alive in order to instill a religious or spiritual grounding in their children. Since we did not produce offspring, our own attachment to this area of life may be far in our past—possibly as far back as our own childhood—or not at all.

A consideration of spirituality should not alienate or exclude agnostics and atheists. Learning and following a spiritual practice without the worship of a deity is a growing phenomenon in the United States and Western Europe. Buddhism, considered a "religion" in the United States, carries a doctrine that is more a practice of meditation and a way of living than a formula for worship. Buddhists recognize teachers and guides, not gods. A Buddhist spiritual life includes a personal exploration of concerns and beliefs, and a regular meditation practice is intended to connect you to a feeling of "one-ness" with something greater than yourself.

Today, many people in the developed world are moving beyond a traditional Judeo-Christian belief system. In the United States traditional houses of worship are shifting and changing to meet the needs of a new generation. In Western Europe, Scandinavia, and the United Kingdom, once heavily Christian areas of the world, the shift is even more pronounced. Many churches have been abandoned and a large segment of the population now claims to live in a "post-Christian era." Traditional Christianity no longer defines their way of life and spiritual practice.

Research reveals that a spiritual or religious practice correlates to an increased sense of well-being in older adults. In pursuit of a satisfying and meaningful life in your later years, consider preparing spiritually as well as physically and emotionally. If you do not have a religious or spiritual practice as part of your life today, and you want to explore this area, Roger Walsh's *Essential Spirituality* is an excellent book on this topic.[16] Walsh explores the principles of all the world's great religions. He extracts from those religions a set of common practices designed to guide people toward a rewarding way of life, a life in which kindness, love, joy, peace, vision, wisdom, and generosity become part of everything we do.

"For me, spirituality includes the belief in things larger than ourselves, an appreciation of nature and beauty, a sensitivity to the world, a feeling of shared connection with other living things, a desire to help people less fortunate than ourselves. All of these things can occur with or without God. I do not believe in the existence of God, but I consider myself a spiritual person in the manner I have just described. I call myself a spiritual atheist. I would imagine that many people are spiritual atheists."

—Alan Lightman, physicist and author of *Einstein's Dream*

---

16   Roger Walsh, Essential Spirituality (Hoboken, NJ: John Wiley & Sons, 2000).

The seven practices, according to Walsh (with my definitions in parentheses) are:

1. Transform your motivation (let go of cravings for and attachment to the material things in life).

2. Cultivate emotional wisdom (learn to feel and express love from your heart).

3. Live ethically (live by a set of values that includes non-judgmental aid and generosity). .

4. Increase concentration (calm your mind; discover mindfulness).

5. Awaken spiritual vision (see the beauty in everyday things).

6. Enrich spiritual intelligence (develop a wisdom and understanding in everyday life).

7. Express spirit in action (become more generous and embrace a service mentality).

Many options are available for exploring spirituality. Some are of a more active nature, involving the whole body as well as the mind: yoga, tai chi, chanting, singing, and dietary routines. Some are more contemplative: journaling, prayer, meditation, artistic expression, and spiritual discussion. Follow the path most appealing to you.

Six Keys to a Fulfilling Older Life Worksheet

Chapters 3 through 10 have described the six keys of a successful older life. The rating worksheet below will give you an opportunity to rate yourself on those six keys. Your score will highlight the areas you may want to work on in the coming years.

Rate yourself on the following: 1 = low, 10 = high

1. How secure are you financially?									
1	2	3	4	5	6	7	8	9	10

2. How active is your pursuit of health and well-being through diet and exercise?									
1	2	3	4	5	6	7	8	9	10

3. How solid is your knowledge of yourself: your values and what brings you meaning and purpose?									
1	2	3	4	5	6	7	8	9	10

4. How flexible are you about what you do and how you live?									
1	2	3	4	5	6	7	8	9	10

5. How do you rate the quality of your relationships?									
1	2	3	4	5	6	7	8	9	10

6. At what level is your interest and/or practice of a spiritual/ religious nature?									
1	2	3	4	5	6	7	8	9	10

What areas do you need to work on to prepare yourself for a rewarding older life?

CHAPTER 11. MAKING AN INCOME IN LATER LIFE

"When you work, you are a flute through whose heart the whispering of the hours turns to music."

—Kahlil Gibran

Have you determined you are not yet financially prepared to rely on your savings and other retirement monies to fund the rest of your life? Welcome to a very big club! The Employee Benefits Research Institute (EBRI) estimates the average accumulated wealth for workers in their fifties and sixties to be less than $150,000.[17] Even when you add in Social Security, that amount will *not* support a twenty-five to forty-year retirement of leisure, volunteer work, and travel—especially if you live in a major metropolitan area. You will need to continue to bring in an income for a few more years. How long will differ dramatically from one person to another. Your financial advisor can give you the most reliable answer.

If you determine you *are* financially able to retire, and you are still holding a job you enjoy and you are in good health, *why* do you want to retire? Are there hobbies, causes, or interests you are itching to pursue? Is there an aging and/or sick relative you need to care for? Are there far-flung exotic places calling out for you to visit? If you can answer with a resounding YES to any of these (or something similar), then by all means, stop working and move on to the next phase of your life. On the other hand, if you were unable to come up with a good reason to leave your job, why not stick with it until you have developed

---

17   Employee Benefit Research Institute and Greenwald & Associates, 2014 Retirement Confidence Survey: Fact Sheet #6: Preparing for Retirement in America, https://www.ebri.org/pdf/surveys/rcs/2014/rcs14.fs-6.prep-ret.final.pdf.

a plan for your post-career years. Continuing to work past the typical retirement age is a perfectly sound strategy. Don't let others dictate when and how you should "retire."

Figuring out what you want to *do* in your second half of life can be a creative and exciting journey. If you want to keep the job you have but want to work less, some employers will let you cut back your hours. Maybe a four-day workweek would give you some much-needed time to visit with an aging parent, get away for long weekends, or simply give you a break from the forty- to fifty-hour workweek. Here's what Jack worked out with his employer:

Jack began contemplating retirement when he reached the eligibility age for his company pension. He had worked as an engineering project manager and spent most of his career at a large aerospace company in the Midwest. He had grown tired of the long workdays and the constant pressure to stay on top of the deadlines, but he didn't yet know how he would spend his time after he retired. Plus, he still had good health and strength. Stopping work entirely felt wrong.

Jack and his wife, Dierdre, wanted to do some traveling once they both left their jobs, and Dierdre was ready to go. She had sold her business the year before and was doing volunteer work in the community to fill her time and feel useful. She enjoyed her life and wasn't nagging Jack to retire, but they had agreed to both slow down in their mid-sixties so they could take trips and do some of the projects they had been putting off for years.

One of Jack's golf buddies told him about how he had begun working part-time for the construction company that had previously employed him full-time. They needed additional accounting help on a seasonal basis, and he was the perfect fit, since he knew all their systems. Jack didn't know of any such program where he worked, but he decided he had nothing to lose by approaching his boss with a similar idea.

To Jack's delight, his boss welcomed the idea. He knew Jack was approaching the age at which he could collect his pension and had been wondering how he would replace him. He had some younger, less experienced project managers, but they needed much more time with the company to understand the systems and get to know the key players. He thought Jack would make an excellent mentor to the younger people.

Jack didn't want to fully retire and his boss didn't want to lose his experience and expertise. Together, Jack and his boss went to the human resources department to find out how to work out the details. They worked out a plan for Jack to take his retirement and come back as a contractor through a temporary agency with whom the company had an agreement. The human resources rep told Jack and his boss that more and more "phased retirement" requests were crossing his desk.

Cutting back your hours will enable you to ramp down gradually over several years. More employers every year are catching on to this excellent way of retaining the knowledge in peoples' heads long enough to pass critical information to younger employees. Like Jack, you may have the chance to be a mentor as you phase out the door in three to five years.

Phased retirement can take many forms and companies in the vanguard of this movement do it in a variety of ways. Kerry Hannon, in "Downshifting the Daily Grind," an April 2016 article for AARP, named Bon Secours Health System in Richmond, Virginia, and Herman Miller, a Michigan-based furniture manufacturer, as representative examples. Bon Secours allows their older employees to gradually reduce their hours or choose less demanding positions in the company. If the move results in a salary decrease, the employee can start to draw their retirement benefits alongside their paycheck. They can also keep their health insurance benefits as long as they work at least sixteen hours a week. Herman Miller offers older employees a "flex-retirement plan," allowing employees to stretch out their retirement over a six-month to two-year period, with gradually decreasing hours. In order to qualify for this plan, the employee must also create a knowledge transfer plan to educate those who are in line to do their work in the future.

> "Yes, money matters, but don't get locked into a must-have salary.... Be sure to account for other benefits, including ...
> - Flexible workday
> - A healthy work-life balance
> - Meaningful work
> - Opportunities to interact with others and stay productive
> - Learning opportunities."
>
> —Kerry Hannon, *Great Jobs for Everyone 50+*

CVS Caremark allows their employees the opportunity to work in different locales at different times of the year when their business experiences a seasonal shift. The most popular transition: a north-to-south migration in the winter months. For example, a CVS Caremark employee in Michigan may put in a request to work in the CVS store in St. Petersburg, Florida for the months of November through April when the St. Petersburg store experiences a bump in their retail trade, warranting this opportunity from a business perspective.

The Aerospace Corporation, an independent, nonprofit company that provides technical analysis and assessment for national security, has a "retiree casual" program to bring back retired engineers. MITRE, another nonprofit organization, has created a "Reserves at the Ready" program.

The above are all examples of the ways companies are helping their employees to retire in stages, so neither the employee nor the employer feels like they are falling off a cliff. Other phasing options may include scheduling alternatives. For example, you may be able to work 20–40 percent fewer hours or compress your work into fewer days. A more radical scheduling shift might include moving to an "on-call" status or doing work by the project, or through job-sharing. By talking to your manager and the human resources department, you may find a way to shift your work status from that of a regular employee to a temp or consultant.

The opportunities for some kind of phased retirement are limited only by your and your employer's creativity and your ability to negotiate areas of importance to you, like continuing your health benefits or maintaining your pension level. If you want to cut back, phased retirement may be worth exploring with your boss.

If you are not working and wondering what you can do with the skills you have and the knowledge you have accumulated over a lifetime, career development help and information is available—in books, on websites, and from workshops around the country. At this point in your life, you have the opportunity to *reinvent* yourself. Nancy Collamer, a career coach and author, has written extensively about finding your calling in the second half of life. In the book *Not Your Mother's Retirement*,[18] she offers the following questions to get you thinking:

- What do you want to spend your days talking about?

- What is the one thing you feel extremely qualified to teach other people?

- What political, global, community, or spiritual issues are most important to you?

- What is something you find easy that others find difficult?

---

18   Nancy Collamer, "How to Reinvent Your Career for Semi-Retirement," in *Not Your Mother's Retirement*, ed. Mark Evan Chimsky (South Portland, ME: Sellers Publishing, 2014), 94-101.

- What are some problems or challenges in your community or the wider marketplace that you'd like to help fix?

- What did you love to do as a child?

- What do you dream about doing (no matter how far-fetched)?

- Whose job would you love to have? Why?

- What can't you stop yourself from doing?

These questions are not meant to provide direct answers to the question "What shall I do?" They are meant to get you thinking along more creative lines about what you have to offer the world. Often, the most appealing and marketable ideas come from a combination of out-of-the-box thinking and a realistic assessment of the skills and knowledge you have gained over a lifetime.

5 MYTHS About Changing Careers in Your 50s

1. It's too late to switch careers

2. It's embarrassing

3. You won't get hired or be able to start a business

4. You'll need to work part-time

5. You won't be able to compete with younger applicants

—Leslie Vos at NextAvenue.com

If you are among the millions of baby boomers needing to work beyond the typical retirement age of sixty or sixty-five, and you are not currently employed, you may need to move away from traditional thinking about how and where to generate an income. Plus, as a person without kids, you may be more flexible than an older parent.

AARP's career website (*aarp.org/work/career-change/*) is an excellent online resource for exploring job and career opportunities. AARP has compiled a fascinating and thought-provoking array of ideas, tools, and resources for finding the right work for you. In addition, you'll find stories and videos of others who have changed their lives by finding new and interesting ways to make a living as an older adult.

Notice I didn't title this chapter "Finding a *Job* in Later Life." Jobs are what come to mind for many baby boomers when they think about earning money. In today's world, a job is much too narrow a vision for how you might earn a livelihood—no matter your age. The world economy has moved well beyond the idea of a "job" being the only way to earn income.

Ever heard of the "gig economy?" It's the twenty-first-century term for earning a living in a non-traditional format. The word "gig" in this context comes from the jazz world of the 1920s. Gig is slang for *engagement*, and is used broadly by musicians of all genres to refer to a paid engagement to play. The term has now been co-opted by the work world to mean paid work, usually of short duration, and not requiring a full-time employment arrangement.

"Free Agent" is another term for the same concept. Consultants are free agents and part of the gig economy. So are charter boat captains, writers, massage therapists, taxi drivers, independent doctors, dentists, and handymen. Free agents are workers who have not become contractually employed full-time. They don't fill out federal W-2 forms. Instead, the money they earn gets reported to the federal and state governments on IRS form 1099. Free agents are then responsible for reporting and paying their own taxes.

The gig economy takes place everywhere and anywhere. Today, if you have a marketable skill you can apply from home, you can do that task almost anywhere on earth. Daniel Pink's 2001 book, *Free Agent Nation*, is a great way to learn more about this relatively new way of making a living.

Temp companies can give you the opportunity to dip a toe into free-agent work. Matching workers with contract work is their business, and many temp agencies have been around for decades. They will help you assess your skills and determine whether you are a candidate for any of the temporary jobs they represent. Of course, they take a sizeable chunk out of what the company pays to hire you, so I suggest moving beyond what they can offer as soon as you get your sea legs in the gig economy. If you are in or near a metropolitan area, Craig's List (www.craigslist.com) provides one of the most popular sources for matching gig work with your skill set.

I often encourage the people I coach to develop a work-life "portfolio." Being a free agent allows you to think of yourself managing a portfolio of endeavors, some of which bring income, while others may be non-income-producing activities that interest you. Portfolio careers are especially attractive to individuals who like variety in how they spend their days. When you are a free agent, you can take on as many tasks as you can juggle. Marlys has had a portfolio career in the photography world:

Marlys describes herself as "independent and resourceful." Over her seventy-one years, she has done many different jobs, but photography is the theme that runs through her life. In addition to her camera work, she now uses her artistic eye to produce events for a museum in Oakland, California.

Throughout her working years, she welcomed new experiences, and her openness led to some fascinating experiences in photography, like being on staff for the Los Angeles Olympics. For a fifteen-year period she produced slide shows for corporate meetings and conferences. From there she got into video, films, and advertising, which landed her a four-year job in the Los Angeles film production industry. After the film industry fling, she worked as a staff photographer at Sunset Magazine, which led to her own show at the Smithsonian. Marlys has no interest in retiring and looks forward to many more years behind the camera.

Shari's story gives us an even more colorful example of a portfolio career. When I interviewed Shari, she told me she had had a "great life." She has "loved everything she has ever done, and doesn't regret one minute or one decision she has made."

At age seventy-five, Shari lives at "River Bend Manor," a well-maintained mobile home park in Reno, Nevada. She moved there over twenty years ago with her third husband, and now considers it her permanent and final home. She volunteered to be on the board of directors for the resident-managed park, but eventually ceded the leadership position to another resident so she could move on and do other things.

In the course of her life, Shari has had more careers than she can count or remember. Her first job was as a customer service rep for Sears, which led to a clerical and administrative job for the Sears Corporation. When she moved from the Midwest to the West Coast in the late 1960s, she started a prepaid legal program for a prestigious San Francisco law firm. She managed that program for seven years and then moved on to manage a dance studio for children, started by a friend.

With her second marriage came a move to Las Vegas, where she managed a car leasing company by day and a strip club in the evenings. In the late 1980s, Shari and her husband moved to Reno. The marriage didn't last, but Shari had started a sign making business which was thriving, so she stayed in Reno. There, in 1991, she met and married her third husband. When they moved to River Bend Manor, Shari intended to finally set down some roots, and she did. She sold her sign business and began working for Safeway, where she quickly earned a promotion to management. Tiring of office work, she became a corporate trainer, ultimately moving into a high-level position in customer relations involving opening new stores in the California-Nevada-Oregon territory.

Eventually, the travel necessary for her job with Safeway became too tiring and she quit. Although Safeway management offered her a "desk job" in Reno, Shari decided to move on. She started selling hats at local festivals, and loved the opportunity to meet people from all over the country. With the local festivals, other people did the traveling and she got to stay put.

Shari became a widow six years ago. She never had children with any of her husbands, not by choice, but because it "just never happened." But like everything else in Shari's life, she has no regrets. She describes her life as fun and varied, and "not yet finished."

Ask yourself, "How much money do I really need at this point in my life?" In this area, those of us without children often have a great advantage over aging parents. Desperately trying to get their kids launched, many older parents are paying off college loans, housing and feeding their twenty- and thirty-something kids, or paying their rent while they hunt for their first jobs. You don't have those burdens. Aiming for an income similar to what you made on your last job can limit your opportunities. Remember, you probably have (or will have) other income sources: a pension or Social Security and a mandatory distribution from your retirement accounts (401k, Keogh, etc.), which will lessen the amount you need to make. Your need for income beyond those sources will be determined by your lifestyle and your budget. Seek out W-2 employment if you like, but remember there are a multitude of other options available today.

The service and hospitality industry has changed dramatically. The "gig economy," also sometimes referred to as the "sharing economy," is responsible for much of that change. Whether we are looking for bargain parking at the airport, help with a party, someone to do yard work, help with a computer breakdown, or a vacation rental, when we need a service today, we go online to find it.

Craig's List, the poster child for the gig economy, was one of the first sites of this kind to go beyond the buying and selling of goods and into the exchange of services. Started in 1995 by self-described "nerd" Craig Newmark, Craig's List began as an email distribution to alert his friends to local events. It quickly gained popularity in the San Francisco Bay Area as a go-to site for announcements and ads, and Craig opened the site to anyone who wanted to subscribe. In 1996, Craig's List expanded into a web-based service, with categories for buying and selling "stuff." Craig ran the company himself until the year 2000, adding job listings and extending its reach to many more metropolitan areas.

By 2012, there were Craig's List sites in over seven hundred cities in seventy countries. Today, on Craig's List you can find almost any (legal) service you can name: handyman, daycare, electronics repair, yard care, moving help, financial analysis and advice, beauty advice, legal help, music lessons, and many, many more. They also list "gigs," the mirror image to "services." People who list gigs are looking for someone to supply the service they need. Examples are domestic help, labor, event workers, art work, videography, and writing. Craig's List's impressive revenue (~$150 million per year) comes from job postings by large corporate employers. This enables them to continue offering its use free of charge for everyone else. Based on their revenue figure, I think we can expect Craig's List to be around for a long time. No better site exists for gaining an understanding of what the gig economy looks like and how people are using it.

Today, quite a number of more specialized sites exist in the gig economy. Task Rabbit (taskrabbit.com) connects people to specific jobs needing to be done. If you think you might like to do some woodworking on the side or be a personal assistant, TaskRabbit might be the right site to advertise your services. Rover.com links dog sitters and dog walkers with people who have dogs to walk. My husband and I use rover.com when we want to go away for a few days or a few weeks and need someone to stay with our pooch. As a dog sitter, you can offer to stay in peoples' homes with their pets or take pets into your home. You can also offer to walk or feed their pets with no overnight responsibility.

If you want to do housesitting, you can choose from a variety of sites advertising home care service for their subscribers. TrustedHousesitters. com, MindMyHouse.com, and HouseSittersAmerica.com are a few popular ones. House sitting can be a great way to take a vacation and make a little money at the same time.

To jump-start your thinking about what you might do to make some income after you leave your midlife career, here are some part- or full-time occupations others have embraced through the traditional and the gig economy:

Opportunities to Get Outdoors

- Dog walker
- Yard worker
- Handyman/woman
- Driver (taxi, school bus, truck, delivery service)
- Coach (soccer, basketball, Little League, etc.)
- School crossing guard

Opportunities to Mingle with People

- Substitute teacher or teacher's aide

- Real estate agent/broker/assistant

- Mentoring/coaching for ESL or young people in school

- Department store clerk

- Grocery retail clerk (Trader Joe's, Whole Foods, etc.)

- Flower and plant shop worker (floral arranger or front desk)

- Personal assistant

- Cooking demonstrator for food companies

- Travel agent or tour company agent

- Tech support rep on-call (e.g., Geek Squad)

- Hotel front desk clerk

- Uber or Lyft driver

- Contract/temp worker in your area of expertise

Opportunities that Keep You on Your Feet

- Bank administrator/teller

- Department store clerk

- Amusement park worker

- Specialty sales in a specialty you love: (hardware, cosmetics, furniture, office supplies, home décor, golf shop)

- Personal trainer

- Coffee shop barista

Opportunities to Make Money from Home

- Seamstress – alterations and/or new garment design

- Writer/blogger/editor/webmaster

- Tutor

- Home-based businesses (Mary Kay, Avon, CAbI, Tupperware)

- Customer service/call center worker

- Medical billing and records clerk

- Virtual assistant and concierge service (by phone and computer)

- Translator

- Instructor of musical instruments (piano, guitar, etc.)

- Virtual agent in your field (physician, attorney, computer tech, mechanic, veterinarian, chef, pharmacologist)

- Tech support – online and by phone

- Marketer of your "stuff" online

- Pet sitter

- Child care

- Maker and marketer of jewelry, paintings, clothing, and other crafts – sell online

Barriers can arise for older workers, and technology is the one I hear about most often. Claudia's odyssey points out how foreign a once-familiar terrain can feel when our work world starts to change.

Claudia, sixty-six, always saw herself as an artist. In college she studied graphic design so she could put her artistic talent to use in a profession that would provide a satisfactory income. The classical training helped her land a job as a graphic artist at a packaging company in the Northeast. She started the job in 1974, got excellent reviews on her design capability and her work ethic, and got herself promoted to a managerial position in 1980. In addition to her design work, she enjoyed managing other artists and helping younger employees adapt to the working world.

In the mid-1980s, things began to change. The company started automating many of their systems and bringing in expensive computers for the design work. Claudia had a hard time understanding how to convert her design skills to a stylus controlled by a computer mouse. On top of her technology struggles, she sensed every engineer and accountant armed with a Macintosh believed they could do her job as well as she. Eventually, her unwillingness to change and her unhappiness at work led to her being "downsized." She went on to three more jobs as a graphic artist, but never fully grasped the computerization of the eight-to-five world. As technology advanced, Claudia felt more and more like a fish out of water. Her last job in the corporate world ended in 2005.

For Claudia, being released from the corporate world felt freeing. Unencumbered by a husband or children, and with a generous severance package from her most recent job, she took time off, taught a few art classes, and pondered what her next move should be.

Eight months after her layoff, Claudia found herself missing the creative part of her work and started to dabble in some new forms of art. She found she was most attracted to jewelry making, and began to create unique earrings and necklaces. At first she gave them away to friends and family members, but when a friend asked if she could pay Claudia to make her a pair of earrings to match the necklace, Claudia realized her art had commercial value.

Today, Claudia has left corporate life far behind. She makes a living from her art, displaying it at festivals and craft fairs around the country. She makes enough money to pay a professional to design and maintain a website and a site on Etsy (an online retail site for artists and craftspeople). That's as far as she is willing to go with computer technology.

If you have been in the workforce in the past decade, you are probably comfortable with a computer and a smart phone. You may, however, need to learn how to use them in different ways. Keeping up with technological changes can be challenging, but abundant help is available. Community colleges, adult schools, city recreation departments, university extensions, and Osher Lifelong Learning Institute (OLLI) chapters offer a wide variety of courses in computer applications and cell phone apps. Going back to school later in life can be a lot of fun and a great way to meet new people. Plus, you will likely find there are as many people in the class like you as there are youngsters! In contemporary terminology, returning to school in one's fifties, sixties, and seventies is HOT.

The topic of work after age fifty deserves an entire book, and indeed many fine ones have been written in the last ten years. You will find several of them, as well as great articles, in the reference section at the end of this book.

"Working," however, is not the only way to bring in income. You may be sitting right now in your greatest asset for income: your home.

At sixty-two, Renee was making a good living at a business she had been passionate about and honed for over thirty years: communication skills training for large corporations around the world. She had her own company, developed her own material, and, being divorced with no children, loved the almost constant travel her work demanded.

Renee had been enjoying doing a robust business until the 2008 recession. In the succeeding years, she noticed she wasn't getting the volume of calls she had once received, and when she reached out to previous clients they told her they remembered her fondly, but as a cost-savings measure they were now putting all their new managers through online training so they didn't have to pay for their employee's or the trainer's travel.

Renee had assumed she would be able to continue to make a living through her training business for another ten years, but the outlook for her work was looking dimmer and dimmer. Recently, while preparing for a business trip to Thailand, she realized she had some free time on the calendar after her training commitment, and decided to stay on as a tourist in Bangkok for three additional days. A friend had told her about a wonderful experience staying in an Airbnb rental, so Renee decided to try it. She booked herself into a room in a private home on the outskirts of Bangkok, owned by an expatriate Irish woman. The home was within walking distance of the metro transit system, so it met her needs and was far less expensive than one of the large Bangkok hotels.

Renee returned home after a wonderful experience with Airbnb, looked around her older, four-bedroom home in Austin, Texas, and asked herself, "Why can't I do that?" She lived close to a transit system that shuttled people back and forth to downtown Austin, and she wasn't far from the University of Texas campus, which, she figured, would yield a constant flow of parents visiting their college scholars, and maybe some of the grad students as well. She relaxed her business marketing efforts and gave Airbnb a three-month trial over the summer.

The trial succeeded beyond her expectations. By the end of the summer, Renee had rented out one or more of her rooms for eighty percent of the nights she made available and had brought in over eight thousand dollars. Plus, Renee had enjoyed every minute of it! Gregarious by nature, Renee loved hosting people from around the world. She made many new friends and received offers to visit people all over the globe. After the trial, Renee asked herself, "If my tired, older house is appealing enough for a $75 per night stay, what might I bring in if I did a major kitchen and bath remodel?" She did some online comparisons with other rooms for rent on Airbnb in her area, ran the numbers, and determined the remodel would allow her to rent her three rooms for $90–$125 per night. It would pay for itself in two years. She went for it.

Renee's life now consists of a little communication skills training and a lot of Airbnb rentals. She also speaks at Airbnb meetings, educating and encouraging others about how to become Airbnb hosts.

I am a big fan of Airbnb, and I have learned by experience you don't have to own a four-bedroom home to be an Airbnb host. Two years ago, I was planning to attend a conference in San Diego. I wanted to find a less expensive place to stay than the $300 per night conference hotel on the waterfront. I also wanted to give myself the chance to get outside and enjoy the beautiful San Diego weather. Looking online, I found an Airbnb listing for $125 per night that suited me.

My accommodation consisted of a private room and bath in a high-rise apartment about a mile from the convention center. My hosts turned out to be a delightful young Australian couple on a work assignment in San Diego for two years. They had a long-term lease on the two-bedroom, two-bath apartment and wanted to make a little extra money on the bedroom and bath they weren't using. They gave me keys to everything, including the health club in the building. I rarely saw them, and when I did we had some delightful conversations about our travels and our families. The arrangement worked out splendidly for all of us. They made a few extra dollars for three nights and I got my exercise and fresh air walking to and from the convention center. I wouldn't have traded it for the finest suite in San Diego!

If you think you would like to give it a try, visit airbnb.com. They will walk you through the steps to becoming a host. You will also find some advice on their site about how to be successful (and safe) as a host.

PART III

DECIDING HOW AND WHERE TO LIVE

Many people begin to get restless in their late fifties and into their sixties. They begin thinking and talking about what life would be like in a warmer climate, in a city center, in a quieter environment, or closer to relatives and friends 'back home.' At some point in your sixties, you may also start experiencing the following: as local friends retire, wind down their careers, and walk their children down the aisle, they begin to depart the old neighborhood in order to move nearer to their kids and grandkids. Those without children don't often anticipate this migratory phenomenon. Grandparenting can become something of a full-time occupation for older parents, which leaves the rest of us in the precarious position of needing to find alternative social outlets. That might involve new friends, a new way of living or a new location.

At the same time, major efforts are underway in many progressive cities and towns to make communities more livable and walkable in order for people to "age in place." Indeed, AARP's research shows the majority of people over fifty want to stay in their own homes.[19] Aging in place is a noble concept, but it may not be the right answer for those of us without children. I urge you to consider all the information about housing and make a conscious decision in a thoughtful, unhurried way.

Determining where to live in your later years should be a two-stage process, dictated by our new longevity. We now have two, and maybe three, phases of "older adulthood," which could last well into our nineties and beyond. The first phase starts in our late fifties or early sixties—about the time many people start to disengage from their midlife careers. At that point, assuming we are healthy, we face some new opportunities.

Being child-free, we have more choices for this early phase. We do not have the added factor of attempting to be near (or move away from!)

---

19   "Survey: What Makes a Community Livable?," AARP website, *http*://www. aarp.org/livable-communities/info-2014/aarp-ppi-survey-what-makes-a-community-livable.html.

adult children and grandchildren. However, if you are married, you still have to negotiate with your spouse and, if your parents are still living or you are close to your siblings, those relationships will impact your choices as well. For many, these choices are complicated. I encourage you to start thinking about what's important to you and discussing your preferences with the key people in your life. Additionally, these decisions are part of two critical objectives for those of us without children: building a community and nurturing a social support system.

The chapters in this section are designed to help you understand the many choices available today. The detailed worksheets will help you sort through your preferences and determine what appeals most to you—at this point in your life and for the future.

Today, not only are there more options for places to move *to*, there are additional options for building or enhancing your social support system that will allow you to remain engaged with people while continuing to live in your own home. These options are good news since isolation and loneliness can creep in rather quickly when we no longer have a *workplace* community. Choosing a place that meets both short-term and long-term needs sets up somewhat of a dilemma. Your early choice may not be appropriate in twenty years, so you find yourself moving again. That's why I encourage you to think of your older adulthood or retirement years in phases or stages and make choices with that in mind.

CHAPTER 12. AVOIDING LONELINESS AND ISOLATION

"Loneliness and the feeling of being unwanted is the most terrible poverty."

—Mother Teresa

Pick up any piece of research on aging, and you will find loneliness and isolation at the top of the list for risk factors to the health and well-being of older adults. Without adult children nearby, we can be especially vulnerable to falling into this unfortunate state. Sometimes a move helps avoid isolation and loneliness; sometimes *not* moving is the way to hang onto those crucial ties to friends and family.

Katie is sixty-three. She retired in May of 2013 from her thirty-year position as a career counselor for a major university in North Carolina. She had earned a decent pension, which she could count on to span the time until she could take her full Social Security at age sixty-six. Katie had never been a homeowner, always renting a one-bedroom condo in Chapel Hill, the relatively expensive area that had been her home for thirty-four years. She had saved money to purchase a home, but never had quite enough to manage a down payment that would leave her with monthly mortgage payments she could afford, so she continued to rent. She had a strong circle of friends there, enjoyed the theater, local museums and other cultural amenities typical of a college town. But now, having retired, she had to live on substantially less income and knew for certain she could not continue to afford Chapel Hill housing prices. Katie had enough money saved to buy a home in a less expensive area, and that desire (a dream she had put off for decades) gave her the courage to make a move.

Katie was born and raised in Pittsburgh, Pennsylvania, and she still had family there. However, she was determined not to live in a cold climate, so she never considered a move back to the Northeast. Katie studied her options for a few weeks, gauging the cost of living, real estate prices, and cultural opportunities in various cities in the Sunbelt, and finally settled on Tucson, Arizona. She made a couple of quick trips to the area, discovered she could easily afford to purchase a nice two-bedroom condo, came home, and started packing.

By August of 2013, Katie had relocated to the Tucson home she had purchased. At first, her new town was exciting and new. Tucson had a university, good shopping, movie theaters, live performances, and most of the cultural amenities she had enjoyed in North Carolina. However, novelty wears off quickly and as the months grew cooler, Katie found the unexpectedly cold winter kept her indoors more than she liked, and her utility costs were higher than she had anticipated. She started playing tennis, but the women in her doubles group lived on the other side of town and seemed uninterested in a friendship beyond the game. She pursued singles groups, hiking groups, and other special interest gatherings, but she didn't have much better luck. On top of everything else, the prevailing political climate in Tucson didn't match Katie's values and beliefs.

"A person's heart withers if it does not answer another heart."
—Pearl S. Buck

Katie had always been an extrovert. She craved the companionship of like-minded women and men. As the crucial spark of connection proved more and more elusive, Katie sank further and further into depression and loneliness. Talking on the phone with friends from Chapel Hill and a few family members in Pittsburgh was her only relief.

By 2015, Katie had made some headway in building a social network that felt supportive and nurturing, but was still far behind where she had hoped she would be. Katie regrets that she hadn't done better research—about the climate year-round, the social scene, the various neighborhoods, the political leaning of the town, and other aspects of her destination—before she turned her life upside down.

Katie's story illustrates how challenging a late-life move can be when one hasn't thoroughly studied and tested the area ahead of time (i.e., made several extended trips at different times of the year). Her experience also highlights how easily even an outgoing and gregarious person like Katie can fall into the trap of loneliness and isolation. Katie has the right personality and understanding of her predicament to know how she got into the situation and is making the necessary adjustments in her life. As of this writing, she has finally found a small circle of friends who show signs of considering her more than a casual acquaintance. Katie is also a *young* older adult. In good physical health at sixty-three, she has the time and energy to seek out new relationships and rebuild a support system for herself.

Katie is one of a very large number of older women living alone. In 2010, seventy-two percent of men over sixty-five were married; forty-two percent of older women were married.[20] Almost half of women over sixty-five live alone. With advancing age, the number and percentage of women living alone takes some profound leaps. Men, who typically do not live as long as women, most often live with a spouse. When they divorce, the majority of them remarry. The older one gets, the more disparate the ratio of men vs. women. The remaining men pair up with the available women, leaving many more women on their own. It can

---

20   Administration on Aging (AoA), US Dept. of Health and Human Services, A Profile of Older Americans: 2011 (Washington, DC: Administration on Aging, 2011).

feel like a game of musical chairs. The chart below gives a breakdown of the living circumstances of men vs. women in 2010:[21]

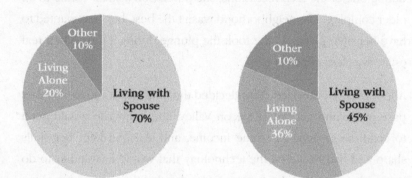

Living Circumstances of Men   **Living Circumstances of Women**

Baby Boomers turn sixty-five at the rate of ten thousand per day. Two thousand of those boomers don't have children, which means the statistics on living alone are certain to get even more pronounced. Isolation and loneliness can follow if we are not careful about our choices. A ten-year Australian study on longevity factors found those with the largest network of friends outlived those with the fewest friends by a significant percentage.[22] Singles are less at risk for isolation than their married counterparts because most singles are content with their lives, know how to take care of themselves, and have built a social support system of family and friends they can rely on. More importantly for those of us without kids, the study found friends—not children or spouses—made the difference.

Moving away from friends and family, even for a long-time single like Katie, can be risky. She found breaking into heavily entrenched social circles challenging. In the following story, Tess provides us with an example of someone who made better choices:

---

21   Ibid.

22   Lynne C. Giles et al., "Effect of social networks on 10 year survival in very old Australians: the Australian longitudinal study of aging," Journal of Epidemiology & Community Health 59(7) (July 2005): 574-79.

Tess, sixty-one, had never married or had kids, and had always lived on her own in Silicon Valley, where she worked. In the early 1990s, during one of the tech recessions, she purchased a small condo in an older complex. The neighborhood wasn't the best, but Tess wanted to have her own place, so she took the plunge during a time when real estate was less expensive.

About twenty years later, Tess decided the time had come to slow her pace of life and get out of Silicon Valley. She knew she would need to continue to generate some income, and she had kept her skills sharp and had mastered the technology that would enable her to do her work remotely (telecommute). She decided the time had come to make a move. Tech was booming when Tess sold her tiny condo and the neighborhood had gotten considerably more favorable over the years. She sold her condo for almost four times what she originally paid. She was now in a great position to buy a small home wherever she decided to go.

Wine had been an interest of Tess for over two decades. She had taken classes to learn more about its cultivation and processing, occasionally helping out at charity wine auctions near where she lived. In addition, as frequently as her budget would allow, she traveled with friends to California's wine country to sample and purchase wines she liked. When the time came to decide where she would move after selling her condo, her passion for the fermented grape heavily influenced her decision. However, wine was not the sole deciding factor. Tess's mother lived twenty miles south of wine country and her brother and his family lived nearby. Moving to Sonoma or Napa County would put her closer to both of them.

Napa County turned out to have real estate prices almost as high as the Bay Area, so Tess decided Sonoma County would be her next home. She found a realtor and made half a dozen trips to the area before deciding on the town she liked, and, finally, the home that felt right.

Although she had made many weekend trips to wine country, Tess didn't have any friends living there. She knew she would have to cultivate a new social network, and that knowledge influenced her choice of a home. With the money from the sale of her condo, Tess purchased a two-bedroom single-family home in Oakmont, a large community for people fifty-five and above.

She loved her new digs from the day she moved in. Even though many of the residents are currently a bit older than Tess, she is nesting into a defined community, one that has many established programs for getting people together. Tess has joined the health club, the singles group, and of course ... the wine tasting club. These connections have jump-started her efforts to make new friends and create a new community for herself.

On weekends Tess sometimes works at one of the nearby wineries, pouring wine for tourists and sharing her expertise about the technicalities of making good wine. She doesn't make much money pouring wine, but she meets a lot of interesting people and the work keeps her in touch with something she loves. Tess also works part-time at her old job, and, thanks to technology, she does her work remotely from her new home. She sees her family regularly, and after ten months has a busy and fulfilling life.

Was Tess *luckier* than Katie? No. Tess was much more familiar with her new locale before she moved and showed some astute foresight in her choice of a fifty-five-plus development. In a retirement community, a significant percentage of the residents are, in a way, starting over, which can be a big advantage to newcomers. Some may have lived in the same town and made a short move to downsize. Many residents, like Tess, have moved there from different towns and different states. Some may be newly single; a few may be newly married. Breaking into established social circles becomes easier when those cliques are not quite as entrenched. Change is frequent, not exceptional, in a retirement community. Tess has met many like-minded women and men who seem eager to form meaningful friendships.

A lack of transportation options is one of the primary reasons for isolation in later life. Statistics tell us half of all non-drivers stay at home when public transportation is more than a ten-minute walk from their homes.[23] Ask yourself the question, "How will I get to the grocery store, doctors, restaurants, or to visit family and friends when I no longer drive?" If there is no public transportation within walking distance from your current home, you run a high risk of isolation. Large, densely populated cities tend to have many more transportation options, so getting around is less likely to pose a problem. If you live in a small town or a sprawling suburb, your community is more likely to score poorly on an accessible public transit test.

If you want to see how your location rates on a walkability index, go to walkscore.com, enter your address, and you will receive a "walk score" from 0–100 for your location. For instance, Boston (a large, densely populated, metropolitan area) has a walk score of 81, number three in the nation for walkability. Austin, Texas (a smaller city where most people live in outlying suburbs), by comparison, has a walk score of 39. In general, the more urban the location, the better the walk score will be. That's due to the density of the population. When it comes to public transportation, the more people per square mile, the more options you will find for getting around without a car and the more likely you will be able to live less than a mile from restaurants, medical buildings, grocery stores, and other essential services.

---

23   Linda Bailey, Aging Americans: Stranded Without Options, (Washington, DC: Surface Transportation Policy Project: 2004). Available at http://www.apta.com/resources/reportsandpublications/Documents/aging_stranded.pdf.

Chapter 13. Privacy, Autonomy, and Independence

"True independence means being free from the domination of your own internal automatic behaviors, not doing what you feel like when the urge strikes."

—Nicholas Lore, Social Scientist and Founder of the Rockport Institute

Your preference for privacy versus connectedness should be one of the key factors in determining where you want to live. Those of us who grew up in the twentieth century—and I assume that includes anyone reading this book—had parents who probably put a high value on *privacy*. Why? It may be because many of our grandparents were immigrants, living in tenements, shared housing, small apartments, or other tiny, close quarters early in the twentieth century. Privacy was hard to find.

Those who can trace their heritage in America back to the nineteenth century or before likely had ancestors who lived on a farm. Farm families were large, out of necessity, and farmhouses were modest. Children often slept two or three to a bed in the few existing rooms. At the dawn of the twentieth century, a newly industrialized America promised work for young people and beckoned people into crowded cities, much like China's industrial revolution today. Those who left the farms were poor at the time, and most of them shared cramped living quarters as they pursued the American Dream and eked out an existence on meager wages.

Around 1950, as we emerged from the Depression and two world wars, Americans found themselves more prosperous. They could afford to put more space between themselves and their extended families and close neighbors. Suburbs began to sprout on the outskirts of every major city and huge numbers of second- and third-generation middle-class Americans were able to buy or rent single-family homes. Even large apartment buildings in New York and Chicago were being constructed with larger spaces and more separation for their new occupants. Ahhh ... privacy at last. With the exception of a handful of hippie communes in the sixties and seventies (a few of which still exist), most Americans have been able to maintain some semblance of separateness from their neighbors ever since.

So, what happens to privacy when we approach our later years? It can be compromised by our need for aid and safety. If you value privacy above almost everything else, you will need to make some early preparations to hang onto it as long as possible. You may also feel a strong need for autonomy or independence. You probably want to keep your driver's license as long as you are physically and mentally fit to drive. You most likely want to maintain control over your own finances and make your own decisions about how to dress, and when, where, what, and with whom to eat.

However, in contrast to the typically American need for privacy and autonomy, *all* of us have a need to be connected to others. We also have a need to be safe and secure. These needs can seem mutually exclusive, yet we must balance them as we get older. This balance will differ dramatically from one person to another. Only *you* can weigh them for yourself as you make your decision about where you want to live as you age.

Advance planning is critical. It may be fine to maintain your independence as long as possible, but consider a later stage of life, one in which you will have needs you are unable to take care of on your own. Boomers are in the first stage of aging. Talking about the later stages can be difficult, but for those who are single or child-free the later stages are where planning is vital.

> **Evaluating your current home or choosing a new one is one of the most important considerations for an older adult. Answering the following questions about your home and your surroundings can be an enlightening exercise:**

The neighborhood

- How would you describe your neighborhood? Can you take a walk around your block safely and easily? Are there sidewalks?

- What do you like about your neighborhood? What do you dislike?

- Do you have neighbors who know you well and would help you in an emergency?

- What is the age mix in your neighborhood? Are there younger families around? If so, do you interact with them?

- Do houses turn over frequently or is the occupancy fairly stable?

- Where is the nearest food store? Pharmacy? Medical center? Shopping mall? Theater?

- If you are still working, can you afford to keep living in your neighborhood when you no longer have an income?

- If you decided to move, what would you look for in your next neighborhood?

The house

- What do you like about your home? What do you dislike?

- How suitable is your home for mobility challenges? If you had knee surgery and were on crutches, would you be able to get to and from your bedroom and bathroom?

- How wide are the doorways? How wide are the hallways? Would they accommodate a wheelchair if you needed to use one?

- What would you need to change about your home to make it more age-friendly?

- If you decided to move to a different home, what would you look for?

These questions are designed to get you thinking about the important criteria for establishing a home as an older adult. The next chapters in this section invite you to look deeper into your preferences for living and give you some idea of what to consider as you age.

CHAPTER 14. DEFINING YOUR MOST IMPORTANT CRITERIA

"Home is a name, a word, it is a strong one; stronger than magician ever spoke, or spirit ever answered to, in the strongest conjuration."

—Charles Dickens

In deciding whether to make a move, we must assess personal needs, do the research, talk with friends, family and/or significant other, and begin to prepare for the future. Some of the terms in this section will be useful to you as you investigate available options in your community (or the one in which you want to live), what you can afford, and what fits your idea of good living. In subsequent chapters you will read descriptions of existing types of communities. They are all worthy of consideration. In addition, I believe we will see a significant number of new living concepts arise in the next ten years, so keep your antenna up for breaking news on housing alternatives.

The worksheet in this chapter is a tool to help you define your personal preferences for housing and the environment in which you prefer to live. It's designed to provide you with a framework for reviewing your desires and needs, and to define what's most important to you in your ideal home and environment. It may be a useful tool in your planning.

Use the worksheet to create a wish list. If you have a life partner or spouse, complete this exercise individually and then compare notes to identify commonalities and differences. Finally, create a common list to capture your agreements as you negotiate them.

Once you have completed this assessment you will have a much clearer picture of the qualities important to you and the location and community that best match your desired lifestyle. You'll have positioned yourself for finding your best home match while minimizing the guessing game and time expenditure in the search.

> **Part A of the worksheet helps you identify the criteria important to you. For example, without pinpointing what kind of geography you prefer, decide whether terrain even matters to you. Continuing with this example, any kind of terrain might be acceptable to you if the location is near your spouse's family. On the other hand, you may find the mountains objectionable to live in, no matter who lives nearby. Use Part A of the worksheet to identify what factors matter to you, and how much they matter.**

PART A: LIFESTYLE AND LOCATION CRITERIA

	Not at all important	Somewhat unimportant	I'm neutral	Somewhat important	Extremely important
Geography— what kind of terrain you prefer (e.g., ocean vs. mountain)					
Climate— how warm/cold it gets, seasonal variance					
Physical setting— what's around you (e.g., suburbs vs. urban vs. rural; transportation options nearby, etc.)					

PART A: LIFESTYLE AND LOCATION CRITERIA

	Not at all important	Somewhat unimportant	I'm neutral	Somewhat important	Extremely important
Cost— affordability of housing					
Proximity to places— easy access to work, theaters, museums, etc.					
Proximity to significant others— family, friends					
Physical space/ type of home— freestanding, condo, one level, acreage, etc.					
Structure and Support Services— planned activities and community-building focus (e.g., 55+, continuous care, cohousing, etc.)					

Having identified your important criteria, Part B of the worksheet provides the opportunity to look deeper into what matters most in these areas. You may want to fill in only the categories you rated as important on the previous worksheet, or you may want to do all of them, even if they are not primary concerns. Some of the terms in this worksheet may be unfamiliar to you at this point, but you will learn more about the different kinds of living options as you read the rest of the chapters in this section.

PART B: LOCATION SPECIFICS			
Geography			
	No way!	I'm neutral	Yes, have to have it!
Coastal setting			
Mountain setting			
Desert setting			
Forest setting			
Flat land			
Rolling hills			
Other:			

Notes:

Climate			
	No way!	I'm neutral	Yes, have to have it!
Hot and dry			
Warm, tropical			
Dramatic seasonal changes with lots of snow			
Moderate seasonal changes with temperate climate			
Other:			
Rolling hills			
Other:			

Notes:

Physical Setting			
	No way!	I'm neutral	Yes, have to have it!
Rural, sparsely populated setting			
Suburban setting			
Urban/city setting			
Has walking trials and bike paths			
In an area regarded as "safe"			
Active adult (55+) community			
Continuous Care Retirement Community (CCRC)			

Notes:

169

Cost			
	No way!	I'm neutral	Yes, have to have it!
Can purchase with cash on hand (no mortgage necessary)			
Is affordable within my specific parameters			
Taxes are lower than what I currently pay (state by state)			

Notes:

Proximity to Places			
	No way!	I'm neutral	Yes, have to have it!
Near my work			
Near museums and galleries			
Near theaters, auditoriums, and event centers			
Near a college or university			
Near good restaurants			
Near my spiritual center or place of worship			
Near public transportation			
Near major airport			
Walking distance to shopping and services			
Near a good hospital			

Notes:

Proximity to Significant Others			
	No way!	I'm neutral	Yes, have to have it!
Family			
Friends			
People with similar interests			
People with similar political leanings			
People with similar spiritual/religious orientation			

Notes:

Structure and Support Services			
	No way!	I'm neutral	Yes, have to have it!
"Village Network" (or something similar) is available			
Access to door-to-curb transportation (for non-drivers)			
Is in a neighborhood with senior-friendly features (pedestrian crossing enhancements, readable street signs, etc.)			
Senior services and a senior center			
Access to planned activites and social gatherings			
Opportunity to step up to assisted living when/if I need it			

Notes:

Physical Space/Type of Home			
	No way!	I'm neutral	Yes, have to have it!
Detached single-family home			
Multi-unit rental (duplex, triplex, small apartment complex)			
Condo or townhome			
Mobile or manufactured home			
Cohousing community			
Rental aparment in a large complext			
Inheritability (an asset I can leave to my heirs)			

Notes:

Home Amenities			
	No way!	I'm neutral	Yes, have to have it!
Privacy			
Attached garage			
Storage space			
Space for overnight guests			
Additional separate unit (casita, in-law, etc.)			
Full kitchen			
Move-in condition (no major repairs or modifications needed)			
Outdoor space for relaxing or entertaining (deck, patio, etc.)			
Opportunity for gardening (flowers, vegetables, etc)			
Exterior maintained by property management company			
Age-friendly safety and convenience features (wide doorways, levers instead of knobs on doors and faucets, waist-level outlets, no stairs, etc.)			
Conforms to my special needs or abilities			

Notes:

Looking at your life in stages can be helpful when thinking about where to live. Using that lens, you can consider what feels right to you now (assuming you are in your fifties, sixties, or seventies) and think about what you will likely want in your oldest years (late seventies, eighties, nineties). In many cases, people end up making two moves, one in their sixties and a second move in their late seventies to mid-eighties when they are no longer up to the demands of living independently. You may be able to avoid this with careful planning, or you may decide you would rather make a second move, if and when necessary, so you can maximize other opportunities for quality of life (like living in a beach town, in the heart of a bustling city, or in another country) for the next decade or two. Chapter 15 introduces the many housing options available for your more active, independent years. Chapter 21 reviews the housing options for the oldest stages of life when living unassisted can be dangerous or difficult. Those may not have relevance or appeal to you at this time, but will be quite important in later decades.

CHAPTER 15. THE EARLY OPTIONS

"Home is where the heart can laugh without shyness."

—Vernon Baker

Those who are child-free and in good health in their fifties, sixties, and early seventies have a multitude of choices for where to live. This chapter contains an overview of the kinds of communities and living options available today. The cost varies greatly by region of the country, so very little pricing information is included. The urban and coastal locales are the costliest, with Midwest and south more modestly priced.

Even though the majority of Americans report wanting to stay in their current homes as they age, research on homeowner satisfaction by the MetLife Mature Market Institute found people who were living in age-restricted "active adult" or "retirement" communities had the "highest home satisfaction rates of all consumers over fifty-five."[24] There are many types of age-restricted communities in the United States. If the idea of living with "a bunch of old retired people" doesn't appeal to you, you should know that only about 10 percent of the residents in these communities are completely retired. Most have active, fulfilling occupations or volunteer careers and have little time to spend on the golf course or in the game room.

Jenny, single and child-free, moved into an age-restricted (fifty-five-plus) community shortly after she turned sixty. She was not even

---

24   MetLife Mature Market Institute (MMI) and National Association of Home Builders (NAHB), Housing for the 55+ Market: Trends and Insights on Boomers and Beyond (New York, NY and Washington, DC: MMI and NAHB, April 2009). Available at https://www.metlife.com/assets/cao/mmi/publications/studies/mmi-55-housing-trends-study-.pdf.

entertaining the idea of retirement at that point in her life; she knew she needed to work at least another five years in order to build up her reserves. However, she wanted to move out of her urban condo and into a smaller community closer to her mother and her two sisters. She looked at a number of subdivisions and developments, both age-restricted and not, finally settling on the former, not because of the age restriction, but because she liked the location and the unit that was on the market. She was excited to purchase a home for herself that was much more spacious than the condo she left.

With many years of experience in trauma unit nursing, Jenny knew she would have no trouble finding a job in her new town, so she made the move as soon as she closed escrow on her new home. That was two years ago. At first, she felt a bit like a fish out of water. She spent most of her first few weeks job hunting and learning her way around. All three hospitals in town offered her a job, so once she decided which of the three she preferred, she started working, which gave her life a routine and a cadence. She made a few new friends at work and visited her mother several times a week.

After eight months or so, Jenny felt reasonably settled. Her mother was doing well on her own and had her own group of friends, so she didn't need Jenny to visit every other day. Jenny decided the time had come to get to know some of her neighbors. She started walking each evening, eventually stopping to chat with some of the other regular evening walkers. Talking led to coffee dates and an occasional movie. Some of her new neighbors encouraged her to get more active in the community, so Jenny joined the singles club and signed up for a yoga class once a week at one of the community center rooms.

Getting to know her neighbors was enlightening. She discovered many of them still worked, either from home or at a more traditional eight-to-five job. She found many had interests similar to hers, and quite a few had moved there within the last five years—making them relative newcomers and the neighborhood less prone to long-standing cliques. After two years, Jenny found herself involved in more activities, with more people, than she had known in twenty years in her previous urban condominium.

Retirement Communities

Retirement communities are age-restricted, meaning all owners or lessees must be fifty-five or older. Where land is not too expensive, these communities can be large, occupying hundreds or even thousands of acres, and have amenities such as golf courses, lakes, and multi-function community centers. The original Del Webb development in Sun City, Arizona, served as the archetype for these retirement communities. Del Webb developments are now sprinkled throughout the United States, with the Sunbelt states of Arizona, New Mexico, Texas, and Florida having the greatest number of them.

As of this writing, The Villages, near Orlando, Florida (thevillages. com), with over seventy-five thousand residents, has the distinction of being the largest retirement community in the United States. As you can imagine, a development of this size looks more like a town than a neighborhood. The Villages and other large developments include stores, fire stations, police stations, gas stations, restaurants, places of worship, movie theaters, transportation, etc. Several other large ones now have health clinics and hospitals within their boundaries as well.

One can either rent or buy single-family homes or condos within these retirement communities. They have appeal for older adults in a wide range of financial circumstances.

Theresa, divorced and child-free, had just turned fifty-six when a large conglomerate acquired the hospital where she had worked as an administrator for twenty-four years. New procedures and guidelines for time accounting and a strict prohibition on overtime led to a falling out with her boss and her eventual resignation. At that point, Theresa decided she had had enough of hospital work and decided to try a new lifestyle. She sold her suburban Maryland home and moved to a midsize retirement community in central Florida. She had several friends who had made a similar move and were quite happy with their decision, so Theresa felt confident a retirement community would provide the opportunity for her to form new friendships, take on a less stressful lifestyle, and take stock of what she wanted to do next.

With the proceeds from her Maryland home sale, Theresa was more than able to purchase a small condominium unit in the retirement community. She combined the remaining funds from her home sale with her modest divorce settlement and invested for the future. She was healthy and knew she would go to work again, but she needed some time to sort out her life and her options. She felt confident that with her hospital pension and some additional savings, she would be able to live comfortably until she could file for her full Social Security benefits at age sixty-six.

During the first few months of her new life in central Florida, Theresa felt a little lost. But after a year had passed, she had gotten to know the area, made some new friends—mainly other single women who had also moved from the Northeast—and had the rudiments of the lifestyle she sought. Her new community had its own library, activity center, golf course, and a large community center with tennis courts and a swimming pool. It also had a transportation system running regularly scheduled vans to nearby stores, several health centers, and the town civic center. Theresa was still driving so she didn't need the transportation system, but knew she might find those vans helpful in the future.

Other than the largest ones, most of these age-restricted communities have no on-site health care, but are often located close to major hospitals and/or health centers. One of the compelling features of selling a home and relocating to a planned older-adult community is the reduction of maintenance responsibilities. In most cases, the monthly fees cover yard maintenance, exterior repairs, and upkeep of all common areas. These kinds of communities are mostly corporate run and managed, with homeowners having little direct say in how things are done and who does them. However, most retirement communities have resident councils or boards, and they can bring significant pressure to bear on management when a repair or upgrade is warranted.

Retirement communities can be an excellent choice for those who are looking forward to giving up home maintenance responsibilities and are looking for an environment in which they can make new friends and participate in organized activities.

Active Adult Communities

Also known as *senior communities* or *active adult lifestyle communities*, these are real estate developments targeted at people over fifty-five. They are age-restricted and have amenities designed to appeal to an older adult. What differentiates them is that they are designed to feel like fancy, expensive resorts, sometimes occupying many acres and including amenities such as swimming pools, gyms, golf courses, natural or manmade lakes, tennis courts, gourmet restaurants, concierge services, transportation, and multi-purpose clubhouses.

People purchase homes in these communities expecting to remain as healthy as possible for as long as possible so they can enjoy the amenities they pay for through hefty association fees. The vast majority of these communities have no on-site health care of any kind. Most of them are corporate owned, with a master plan. Two excellent examples are Robson Resort Communities (robson.com) and Trilogy Active Lifestyle Communities (trilogylife.com). Like the simpler, less costly retirement communities, you will find most of the active adult communities in the Sunbelt states, though you will now find quite a few in the Northeast, the Midwest, and the Pacific states as well. Developers of these kinds of properties are well aware that living near family often trumps a more hospitable climate, so you can find them in or near almost every metropolitan area of the United States.

Like retirement communities, an active adult community can also be an excellent choice for older adults without children. If the price fits your wallet and a well-maintained, amenity-rich environment appeals to you, this may be the right option. Joanne made that choice.

Joanne lost her husband, Jim, to cancer when they were both fifty-eight. They had been the quintessential double-income-no-kids couple, working in Chicago and living in an upscale community of working professionals with easy access to downtown via the Chicago transit system. They had enjoyed season tickets to the Chicago Bulls games and the symphony, and often stayed in town on weeknights to attend theater productions. They rode their bikes and played tennis on summer weekends, and took several memorable vacations to Europe and the Caribbean Islands.

After Jim's death, Joanne continued to work for a couple of years, but her life felt different. She and Jim had begun talking about what they might do in retirement, where they would travel, where they would live, and when they might be able to afford to quit their jobs. Without her partner, Joanne didn't know which of those plans and discussions had meaning for her anymore.

Jim and Joanne had married shortly after college and done almost everything as a couple. After Jim's death, their friends—all couples—treated Joanne kindly, but after a few months the invitations to dinners and backyard barbecues stopped coming. The only social outlet Joanne had were the friendships she had made at work and one divorced sister who lived twenty minutes away. After a discussion with her financial advisor, Joanne decided to search for a community that would provide her with a lifestyle free of maintenance duties and lots of options for active living.

The one thing Joanne didn't lack was money. Jim's company had offered a generous benefit package to its executives, and early in his career Jim had taken out a life insurance policy as well. Between her spousal benefit from Jim's pension and the handsome life insurance settlement, Joanne knew she could choose to retire any time she liked, so at sixty-two, she gave notice to her company and started to look around for what she would do next.

Joanne spent her first six months of retirement traveling to various active living retirement communities. Her search led her to a community in Broomfield, Colorado, between Denver and Boulder, which had every amenity she could imagine and more. She made three trips to visit, each in a different season, and settled on a mid-level resale home near the clubhouse with its four tennis courts.

Upon moving to Broomfield she discovered some of the residents in her new community were still working, while others were fully retired. Within the first few months, she knew she had made the right decision. She worked out daily in the fitness center, joined the women's tennis club, and became friendly with several single women who shared her enthusiasm for the outdoors.

In her eighth month in Broomfield, one of her new friends asked if she would be interested in doing some volunteer work at a nearby school that needed help in the library and their after-school programs. Joanne liked the idea of taking on something that challenged her mind as well as her body, so she said yes. Today Joanne splits her time between activities in her retirement community and the school where she teaches tennis to seventh and eighth graders in their after-school program.

Here's a way to start researching retirement communities and active lifestyle communities from the comfort of your desk chair: take a look at the website 55places.com. The site allows you to search by state and get a good feel for the location, prices, and amenities these communities have to offer.

Cohousing Communities

Cohousing is another alternative gaining ground today. Cohousing communities are developed and managed by the resident owners, rather than by large corporations. They have far fewer amenities, so if swimming pools and golf courses are critical for you, these small, grassroots communities seldom come with that kind of package.

If you are tempted by the idea of joining some of your friends to design a small living cooperative for your later years, cohousing may be the concept you are looking for. The Cohousing Association of the United States *(cohousing.org)* describes the idea as follows: "Cohousing is a type of collaborative housing in which residents actively participate in the design and operation of their own neighborhoods. Cohousing residents are committed to living as a community. The physical design encourages both social contact and individual space. Private homes contain all the features of conventional homes, but residents also have access to extensive common facilities such as open space, courtyards, a playground and a common house."

The origins of cohousing can be found in Denmark, where the concept is still alive and well. Cohousing got its start in the United States about thirty years ago, as a way for families to share the work and fun of raising kids in a common development, where everyone knew everyone else and took part in the process. Today, however, thanks to the boomer population, there are "senior" cohousing communities as well as multi-generational communities, both in existence and in the planning stages.

Cohousing can be an excellent choice for community-minded seniors. The concept is less familiar to most people than the previous options, so I'm including a more thorough description:

According to the Cohousing Association of the United States, the six "defining characteristics" of cohousing are:

1. A Participatory Process. Future residents design the community to meet their unique needs. Future residents work closely with the developer or architect to design exactly the space they want.

2. Neighborhood Design. The physical layout and the orientation of the structures on the site encourage a sense of community. Dwellings usually face each other and are clustered close together to allow maximum shared open space. The common house is the focal point and visible to every resident from their home. Parking is often on the perimeter, with no private garages. Design can vary, but the intention is to foster a strong sense of community, facilitated by design.

3. Common Facilities. The common house is designed for daily use and considered an important supplement to the private residences. The structure usually includes a common kitchen, dining area, laundry, and sitting area. In multi-generational cohousing communities, there will also be a playroom for the children. Depending on the budget of the community and the

scope of what they envision, the common area may also include a library, craft area, workshop, exercise room and one or more guest rooms. With the exception of tightly confined, urban sites, cohousing communities almost always put a great deal of emphasis on the open space, often designing garden plots, walking paths, play areas, etc. Since the buildings are clustered, the open space might be several acres of undeveloped space.

4. <u>Resident Management.</u> Residents manage the community and perform the lion's share of the maintenance work required. They participate in governance, developing policies that must be agreeable to all, and meeting regularly to air and resolve problems. One of the key functions is a participatory community meal program, which occurs at least once a week.

5. <u>Non-Hierarchical Structure and Decision-Making</u>. Most groups start with a few "burning souls" who are the initial evangelists of the project. As more people join, each individual takes on a role commensurate with her/his abilities and interests. Most cohousing groups make all decisions by consensus, with no individual having an opinion that outweighs the others. Most communities have a voting policy that goes into effect if a decision cannot be reached through consensus, but in existing communities, resorting to voting has been rare.

6. <u>No Shared Community Economy</u>. The community should not be a source of income for its members. Occasionally, a cohousing community might pay one of its residents to do a specific and unusual task, but these kinds of things are usually considered the member's contribution.

As with most of the other options mentioned here, a cohousing community does not include any provision for medical care or paid help with the activities of daily living, should you need such care. However, the commitment within these communities to helping each other through life's passages amounts to a strong inclination to lend a hand in times of need. When a cohousing community member needs help with care after surgery or during debilitating treatment like chemotherapy, other members typically organize care cooperatives, food deliveries, and companionship.

If the idea of a *senior* cohousing community intrigues you, I recommend taking a look at the following communities: Washington Village in Boulder, Colorado (washington-village.com), Wolf Creek Lodge in Grass Valley, California (wolfcreeklodge.org), or Westwood Cohousing in Asheville, North Carolina (westwoodcohousing.com). Cohousing is experiencing increasing appeal among baby boomers and although in some cases they cannot be legally age restricted, many in development today are designed to appeal much more to older adults than to young families. The Mountain View Cohousing Community (MVCC) in Mountain View, California (about forty miles south of San Francisco, near Palo Alto and Stanford University), is a great example of an adult-oriented cohousing community. Here is their story:

> MVCC opened in late 2014, but the original vision for the community dates back to 2006. It started as the dream of Susan and David Burwen, long-time residents of Mountain View and empty nesters. They began that year to share their vision of an older-adult cohousing community with friends and colleagues and to recruit others to join in the effort.

> Vacant land is expensive in Mountain View and Palo Alto, and the fledgling team of cohousers was not finding a suitable piece of property on which to build their new home. Finally, in 2009, during the deepest part of the recession, the Burwens and other founding members were able to purchase a piece of land large enough to build the community they had in mind. Plans were eventually approved by the City of Mountain View in 2011 and groundbreaking followed in the summer of 2013.

> During those intervening years, the membership of MVCC grew and changed as one would expect, with the end result that exactly half of the original group from 2007-2008 became the initial owners and are now residents. Bi-monthly meetings and monthly potlucks held the community together and nurtured the bonding process during the years before they had a cohousing home. Members were involved in

the planning of the project and played an active role in making the many decisions required throughout construction. Through shared commitment to community and trust-building, the dream came to fruition—for the Burwens and the entire community.

The property MVCC purchased was not a completely vacant lot. In the back corner of the one-and-a-half-acre site, was a small, dilapidated farmhouse. Having been told by the City of Mountain View that the structure was on the historic register and they could not tear it down, the building design committee decided to refurbish it and turn the Victorian-era cottage into a guesthouse. Today, it is beautifully restored, and serves as quarters for visiting family and friends. However, the long-term vision is that the farmhouse will be dedicated to housing for one or more caregivers for members who become frail or ill.

A cohousing community, either multi-generational or adult-focused like the one in Mountain View, can be an excellent option for collaboration-minded singles or couples. Although most of the members in MVCC are older parents, those among them without children are developing strong ties to other members, and, in some cases, to other members' adult children living nearby. The current age spread of MVCC owners is mid-fifties to early eighties, though that demographic will likely change when units turn over.

I visited MVCC in the summer of 2016 and found a fully functioning community. The members share three meals a week prepared by a rotating core of cooks and helpers, watch movies in the media room, take care of the property with little help from outsiders, and maintain a beautiful guesthouse for the members' families and other guests. In addition, 2016 marked the first year the raised-bed vegetable garden was ready for planting, and by the time of my visit it was yielding enough food for most of the common meals, with extra available to members for their private meals. By mid-July, the tomato plants were a deep healthy green, taller than I, and bearing hundreds of pieces of fruit—a testament to the dedication and work of several experienced gardeners and an abundance of compost, contributed by all of the nineteen households.

The cohousing concept appealed to Anna and Greg:

> Now in their late fifties, Anna and Greg have lived in a cohousing setting since the completion of their community in 2014. They were both born in Taiwan and, as young people, traveled to the United States to study and settle if they found good jobs. They didn't know each other in Taiwan; they met in the United States in a church choir. Their histories, however, were familiar to one another. They were each the middle child in their families, so neither had been pressured to stay in Taiwan with family or take care of parents as they aged. That gave Anna and Greg the freedom to live their lives as they desired, where they desired.
>
> They were married in 1986 and bought a large home in a Silicon Valley suburb. Initially, Anna and Greg wanted children, and Anna tried for several years to get pregnant. In their mid-thirties, they tried in vitro fertilization, but it did not work. By the time they had reached their forties, they decided to enjoy life as it was, without children, a decision acceptable to their Taiwanese families, since they both had siblings who had produced heirs to carry on the family line. They also knew they would never move back to Taiwan.
>
> As they got into their fifties, they started losing family members. Every year, one or the other had to go back to Taiwan to visit with an aging parent or attend a funeral. They also noticed older family members in Taiwan being cared for by their daughters or sons. With few relatives in the United States, Anna and Greg realized they needed to build some kind of community around them.

In 2009, Anna saw a local TV clip featuring a groundbreaking ceremony for a local cohousing community. Anna made note of the website, went online and registered for email updates. Anna and Greg also discussed the idea of starting their own cohousing community with some friends, but the concept didn't have much appeal to anyone in their social circles.

In 2011, they joined an organized tour of several San Francisco Bay Area cohousing communities, many of which had been in operation for over ten years. Meeting people already living in cohousing and hearing their stories of working together to build a close and caring community finally tipped them over the edge. They applied for membership in the one that seemed most appealing, and joined a fledgling community. The building would not be ready for occupancy for another eighteen months, but cohousing is a do-it-yourself project from start to finish, and although a local builder was erecting the structure, the members—residents-in-waiting—had scores of decisions to make at every juncture. Plus, the years leading up to actual occupancy in a cohousing community are a time for bonding, community-building, and learning to make decisions together.

You can find out much more about cohousing, cohousing architects, or search for available homes in existing communities at *cohousing.org*.

Home Sharing

Remember the 1980s Emmy-winning TV sitcom, *The Golden Girls*? The ensemble cast (Betty White, Bea Arthur, Rue McClanahan, and Estelle Getty) played older single women sharing a home in Miami. Rue McClanahan's character, widow Blanche Deveraux, owned the home and placed a "room-for-rent" ad on the local bulletin board. Widowed

Rose and divorced Dorothy, the characters played by Betty White and Bea Arthur, answered the ad and moved into the house along with Dorothy's eighty-year-old widowed mother, Sophia, played by Estelle Getty. The show often focused on the inevitable disagreements over everything from food to clothing to décor, yet one couldn't miss how, over seven seasons, the women grew to care deeply for one another. They helped and supported each other through love affairs, sickness, heartaches, and deaths.

One day in 2013, at a conference featuring new ideas for aging, I met a woman who told me about the ups and downs of her own Golden Girls-style home. Her tales included the story of one roommate who needed surgery and an ensuing five-month rehabilitation period. The other three women in the house signed up to be her advocates in the hospital, and helped her through the rehabilitation period at home. Without the help of the housemates, the one who needed care would have been in a much more precarious position, needing to hire outside caregivers or move into an expensive rehab facility for several weeks. She shared with me that the incident and its aftermath brought the housemates closer together, each recognizing how easily it could have happened to any one of them.

The idea of replicating *The Golden Girls* theme has taken hold in the minds of many others, both men and women, and several innovative organizations have sprung up in the last few years to facilitate matching of those who have a home and those who need a home and want to live with others.

SeniorHomeShares.com bills itself as an online matching service. Homeowners and home-seekers both fill out a personal profile, including a unique description of the kind of home they have to offer or what they are looking for, as well as their budget and location. SeniorHomeShares.com then applies an algorithm to identify promising housemates, which they present to their users on an ongoing basis, very much like a dating site. Users can then exchange messages through the company, which are forwarded to their personal email. For those who are uncomfortable with technology, they provide several options: users may include a "helper" for their account. The helper could be a friend or family member. They also provide phone support, which is staffed by older adults who are familiar with the system and sympathetic to the challenges technology presents to some users.

Silvernest (Silvernest.com) is another rapidly growing home sharing service for baby boomers, offering a roommate matching website for older adults and boasting over seven thousand users in their first year of operation. Silvernest's home page features an attractive and informative video to introduce their services, and it utilizes the most up-to-date technology to help people find just the right home to share with others. Silvernest also offers help with the screening process and the contractual arrangements for those offering to share their home. In addition, they facilitate secure communication between prospective renters and homeowners through the back end of their website, enabling people to get to know one another safely before they share personal information. For those who are seeking a room to rent, Silvernest offers mapping technology, much like you would find on a hotel search site like TripAdvisor.com or Expedia.com. They also offer background checks, lease agreements, and direct deposit of rent checks once the tenant relationship begins.

Home sharing can work well for singles, providing a built-in social outlet as well as a safety net for short-term setbacks like the one described above. In the long term, a shared home is rarely a perfect solution, but can be an excellent alternative to becoming isolated in a house or apartment when you are in your sixties, seventies, or beyond.

Intentional Communities

For some, the pursuit of community becomes intertwined with their spiritual interests or their lifestyle. An "intentional community" is a living arrangement developed around a lifestyle choice, a spiritual practice, or a common background of the residents. They generally take the form of a housing cooperative or cohousing community. The oldest example of this kind of community can be found in the Catholic traditions of nuns and friars who pledged obedience to a particular order and lived in a practicing community.

Today there are a number of examples that go well beyond a particular religious tradition. *Pilgrim Place* in Claremont, California is a senior community for those who serve (or have served) in religious or charitable organizations for most of their lives. Those who are attracted to the community want to live in an intellectually stimulating environment offering them the chance to continue to serve and explore opportunities for spiritual growth and learning. Residents include ordained missionaries, professors of religion, YMCA/YWCA staff, community organizers, and peace and justice advocates. Their lifestyle design is similar to a continuous care retirement community.

Asheville Mountain Meadows in Mars Hill, North Carolina, is a green, organic, and sustainable community established in 2009. The earliest residents started living there in 2012. And they are growing as people discover them, purchase a lot, build a home, and become permanent members of the community. They are organized around dynamic governance, and are committed to working the land and fostering positive, fruitful, and conscious relationships with one another.

The *Burbank Colony* near Hollywood, California, is a senior artist colony. With a professional theater group under its roof and college-quality classes in everything from filmmaking to watercolors, the

Burbank Colony attracts older artists of all types, offering them a home in a creative community. All of its living units are rentals.

Elder Spirit (ElderSpirit.net) was one of the pioneers in the cohousing movement. They are a great example of an intentional community paired with the cohousing concept of governance. For more information on the concept of intentional community, take a look at the Fellowship for Intentional Community's directory (ic.org).

A different kind of intentional community is an RV (recreational vehicle) park, and Jojoba Hills Resort in Southern California is a good example. Jojoba Hills SKP RV Resort is an active, over fifty-five community, and is part of the Escapees RV Club (SKP for short). Membership at Jojoba Hills is open to anyone who is already a member of SKP and meets the age requirement. It is also dependent on the availability of a site (a 50' x 70' concrete pad and storage shed), for which there is usually a waiting list.

Jojoba Hills has amenities resembling a fancy retirement community: a pool, two spas, a clubhouse, library, exercise room, pool and card room, a craft room, and a tennis court that converts into four pickleball courts. The resort maintains full-time staff that reports to an elected board of "member" directors. Run as a cooperative, volunteerism by members is crucial to its success, and most members participate in whatever way they are able. Jojoba Hills' proximity to San Diego and Los Angeles makes it convenient to shopping, theater, and fine dining. Most members consider the resort their "home base" and use either their main RV or a secondary RV to travel for some portion of the year.

Frances and Paul have been members of the Jojoba Hills community for four years and plan to spend the rest of their lives there. At sixty-one and sixty-seven, they are not yet fully retired. Frances works as a recruiter and staffing consultant; Paul is a musician. Their previous careers were in human resources (Frances) and as an EMT (Paul). Their union is a second marriage for both of them and they wanted a fresh start, so they decided to leave the expensive metropolitan area where they had each spent the last thirty years and take up the "vagabond life," as Frances calls it. They considered a sailboat, but ultimately decided an RV would be more practical.

Selling their home and divesting themselves of a lifetime accumulation of stuff took them the better part of a year. They then rented several different RVs and travel trailers for short trips to try out various sizes and styles. They settled on a thirty-foot rig, made the purchase, and set out on their adventure.

Without family to rely on, they both understood well the value of having a community around them, so as they traveled around the country, they were on the lookout for a place to call home when they weren't on the road. When they stumbled upon Jojoba Hills, they knew they had found their community. Today, four years into their new lifestyle, they are finding they need to spend more time at "home" (Jojoba Hills) than they originally planned because Frances needs reliable Internet access to run her consulting business and Paul needs to develop relationships with the clubs, nearby wineries, and other venues that might hire him to play music for their events.

They found gasoline to be the single biggest expense of their vagabond lifestyle, so they purchased a second, smaller RV for traveling, and permanently parked the original RV on their pad at Jojoba Hills. All in all, the vagabond life is far less expensive than owning or renting a home. Frances and Paul no longer worry about running out of money or finding a community in which to live. They plan to do more traveling in about six years when they are both retired, but now they are content to hang out in their Southern California home and take long weekend trips in their smaller rig.

If Frances's and Paul's lifestyle appeals to you, you can find out more about life on the road at rvwheellife.com, wheelingit.us, and roadlesstraveled.us.

Continuous Care Retirement Communities (CCRCs)

Continuous Care Retirement Communities, or CCRCs, as they are often called, are a kind of middle ground between the earlier living options in this chapter and the later options discussed in Chapter 21. In my opinion, CCRCs are among the best choices for those without children, since they satisfy the needs for safety, security, community, and care that an older adult may need. However, CCRCs are expensive, so they are not an option for everyone. The high move-in costs and pricey maintenance fees are reasons many people wait until they are in their late seventies or eighties to make the move. Even the well-heeled don't want to make those steep monthly payments for three decades, especially if they are buying services they do not yet need.

My in-laws moved into a CCRC in Florida when they were in their mid-eighties. Shortly thereafter, we visited them and stayed in the facility's guest suite. When I asked them how they liked living there, they sighed and told me, "We love it; we wish we had done it ten years earlier." A handful of people move into CCRCs in their late sixties, often with older spouses. They generally find that entering the community at a relatively young age gives them a lot of time to take advantage of the many amenities CCRCs offer and to develop a community of friends. If you can afford it, a CCRC is worth considering at any age beyond fifty-five. The majority of residents move in when they are in their seventies. We will discuss CCRCs in much greater depth in Chapter 21.

Cultural Specialty Communities

Some developers are discovering niche markets for older adult communities. Shantiniketan is a community for older Indian-Americans in Florida. Shantiniketan opened in 2010 and gained popularity so rapidly that it is now expanding.

Fountaingrove Lodge, an upscale active adult development with an option for continuous care opened in Santa Rosa, California in 2013. Heavily marketed to the LGBT community, the development became an immediate success and now claims to have a five-year waiting list. The residential make-up at this time reports in at 70 percent LGBT and 30 percent straight older adults.

Tina, a single gay woman, moved to Fountaingrove Lodge in late 2013. Prior to her move she had been living near Santa Cruz, a coastal town south of the San Francisco Bay Area. Santa Cruz had been LGBT-friendly for many years. Tina felt comfortable there and had a community of close friends. Earlier in her life she had had a couple of serious relationships, but they hadn't worked out and now Tina has been single for over twenty years.

As Tina moved into her late fifties, she began to question what she could do to ensure herself comfort and security in her later years. She had reason to be concerned: her mother, grandmother, and great grandmother all developed forms of dementia as they got older. Both of her parents lived into their late eighties, and as they became less able to protect themselves from scam artists and make their own decisions, Tina had taken over the management of their finances. Playing that role in her parents' lives made her realize how vulnerable she would be on her own.

Tina decided she had to make some strategic moves in her own life. Purchasing long-term care insurance was the first action she took.

Her father had purchased it when he was in his fifties and had used the benefits for a year and a half before he died. For a single person, long-term care insurance seemed like a smart investment. She also began looking around for a place to live out her life—one that offered a system of graduated care if and when care became necessary. Being well-connected with the LGBT community in Santa Cruz, she received notice of the opening of Fountain Grove Lodge, drove up for a visit, and made her decision.

Tina has been at Fountaingrove Lodge for three years now and is glad she made the move. Fountaingrove has a younger average age (seventy-four) than most CCRCs, probably due to the nature of their target market. Most of the residents are still quite active, which provides more opportunities to connect with others and form relationships.

CHAPTER 16. STRANGER IN A STRANGE LAND: MOVING TO A DIFFERENT COUNTRY

"Twenty years from now, you will be more disappointed by the things that you didn't do than by the ones you did do."

—Mark Twain

Spending one's later years outside the United States, whether to save money, live in a more hospitable climate, or for the adventure, has become more and more attractive in the last twenty years. The lure of year-round tropical breezes, coupled with a cost of living that can be as little as one-quarter what one would spend in the United States has been irresistible for many. More than a half million Americans over the age of sixty-five now have their Social Security payments mailed to addresses outside the United States.[25] Life abroad can be particularly appealing to those who don't have to worry about seeing grandkids grow up. The following story involves a couple who experienced some unexpected setbacks that ultimately led them to a rewarding life outside the United States.

In 2000, Diane and Greg were in their early fifties, enjoying their lives as a child-free professional couple in Northern California. Diane was an organizational consultant and derived a secondary income as a distributor for a company that published personality assessments and sold their products through a multi-level marketing program. The company had an excellent reputation, and had been in business for

---

25   Shelley Emling, "This is What Retiring Abroad Looks Like," Huffington Post, March 2, 2015. Available at http://www.huffingtonpost.com/2015/03/02/what-retiring-abroad-looks-like_n_6762974.html.

over twenty years. Diane used the popular products herself, as did many in her field. Plus, she had gotten into the program early and had built a sizeable "down-line." (If you are not familiar with multi-level marketing, the way people earn money over and above their own sales commission is by recruiting other people into the system to sell the products. Those recruits then become their "down-line," and they receive a small cut from anything the down-line rep sells). As a down-line "manager," Diane received a percentage of everything her down-line reps sold, as well as a percentage of her down-line recruits' sales. Diane had been proactive in building her down-line over the years, recruiting younger reps and supporting them as they built their own businesses. She made good money and was counting on the passive income for her retirement.

Greg had a promising retirement outlook as well. He had over twenty years of service as a highly trained sheet metal mechanic for a San Francisco-based air carrier. Greg always enjoyed his work, but repairing and replacing airplane siding requires both strength and experience. Greg had the latter, but at fifty-one, his strength was starting to wane and he was looking forward to the pension he was owed when he hit twenty-five years with the company.

Greg and Diane took the first step toward retirement in 2002 by selling their California home and relocating to the Las Vegas area. Greg commuted weekly back to his job in San Francisco. Meanwhile, Diane began to ramp down her work to spend time with Greg when he retired the following year. They wanted to be able to live comfortably on Greg's pension and Diane's income from the down-line, do some traveling, and enjoy the fruits of their labors.

Over the next five years, fate handed Greg and Diane a double whammy. The first blow came in 2003. Hidden in the fine print of Diane's contract was the provision for the publishing company to change its sales and distribution structure at any time. In one stroke of the pen, the company did away with their multi-level marketing system, converted to a more traditional sales structure, and wiped out Diane's passive income.

The second blow came in 2005 when, after four tumultuous years, the airline, in the wake of their Chapter 11 bankruptcy filing, cancelled their pension plan. The default was the largest in US corporate history, with Greg one of several thousand victims. Thanks to more recent legislation, today that company's action would be illegal, but the congressional action wasn't in time to save Greg's pension.

Greg and Diane were devastated, but they also proved to be resilient. In 2006, they purchased a good-sized trailer home which could be pulled by Greg's pickup, and started looking for a less expensive place to settle. Their search led them to the Baja Peninsula of Mexico. They started with a month to see if life in Baja suited them. In the following years, one month became three, and then five. Diane and Greg found they were spending almost no time at all in their Las Vegas area home, so they sold it. They are now full-time residents in a delightful mobile home community about forty miles north of Cabo San Lucas.

When I visited them a few years ago, Greg was out fishing with some buddies and Diane was finishing a webcast for her consulting business. Greg no longer works, but Diane continues to work from their home—not because she has to, but because she enjoys the work and can now do it from their home in Mexico. Their cost of living is extremely low, well covered by their Social Security and Diane's continuing income. They have built a strong social network in their tight-knit community, and the dental and medical clinics in the area are quite good. They travel back to the United States twice a year to see family, but their life is now firmly entrenched in their adopted country.

Because of recent changes and the downturns in the US economy, Greg and Diane's story has been repeated thousands of times, by couples and singles in similar circumstances. AARP did a study in 2010 to find the "best" places to retire abroad.[26] The criteria were simple: good-to-excellent health care, attractive locale, affordable, and safe and hospitable to older Americans. The following locations made the short list (in no particular order):

- Buenos Aires, Argentina

- Corozal, Belize

- Central Valley, Atenas, Costa Rica

- Languedoc-Roussillon, France

- Le Marche, Italy

- Puerto Vallarta Region, Mexico

- Granada, Nicaragua

- Boquete, Panama

- Cascais, Portugal

- Costa del Sol, Spain

There are many other enticing locations, especially in the Western Hemisphere. Mexico seems to be the destination of choice for many California expatriates. San Miguel de Allende and Lake Chapala, near Guadalajara, both have large expatriate communities, as do the coastal towns of San Jose del Cabo, Puerta Vallarta, Mazatlan, and others. Friends and colleagues I have visited seem quite happy and content in their new countries.

Enticements other than money can herald the call to live abroad. Dana's motivation came from a need to be near family.

---

26   Barry Golson, "Paradise Found," AARP The Magazine (September/October 2012). Available at https://www.aarp.org/home-garden/livable-communities/info-07-2010/paradise_found.html.

At seventy-three, Dana decided to restart her life in France. She was strong and healthy and had recently divorced after thirty years of marriage. Without the anchor of children or grandchildren, she had no compelling reason to stay in the Ohio town where she had made her home since college.

France was familiar to Dana. When she was eight years old, her parents moved the family to a town on the outskirts of Paris, where they remained until they passed away. Dana had returned to the United States to attend university. Her younger sister, however, married in France and remained there to work and raise her children.

Dana had been a professional graphic artist, creating fine art on the side, more for the love of it than for any monetary gain. She did well at her graphic art and made a name for herself in the local area. However, after the divorce, she took stock of herself and her situation and realized she didn't want to grow old so far away from the younger sister she loved and the nieces and nephews she adored. She decided to make the move back to France, and her financial advisor helped her work out the details of how she would sustain herself in her new environment.

Dana now lives in Aix-en-Provence, in the south of France, not far from her sister. Because of her youth in France, she has dual citizenship and gets health care coverage through the French Social Security system. When she is not playing aunt to her nieces and nephews, she spends her time painting and drawing, occasionally selling a piece, which gives her a small income in addition to her US Social Security check. Dana has discovered aging in France to be easier than in the United States due to the many social programs that support the older population. It also helps that she speaks both English and French.

She misses her friends in Ohio, but thanks to Skype and other modern technologies, she talks with them often and shares tales of her new life in her re-adopted country.

When asked whether they would consider moving out of the US later in life, many people express concern over health care. They wonder if they would get the same level of care in another country as they would in their Medicare program. In fact, in a recent Harvard Public Health survey, 72 percent of respondents expressed a favorable opinion of the federal health program for older adults. However, as Richard Eisenberg points out in a follow-on article about the study, Medicare doesn't always stack up favorably against health care abroad.[27] Chief among the findings on that report is that US seniors are more likely to be sick and have trouble affording care than those in "peer" nations. Other key findings were:

- In Canada, the Netherlands, and the United Kingdom, there are no deductibles or cost sharing for primary care.

- Many older Americans worry about having enough money for their medical needs; similar worrying is far less prevalent in comparable countries.

- Over 20 percent of older Americans reported spending more than $2,000 in the last year on medical costs. In all other countries surveyed, fewer than 10 percent spent that amount or more.

Where Medicare does excel is with preventive care and encouragement to stay healthy, so if you decide to live abroad, you will have to be self-motivated and take charge of your own wellness.

---

27   "How Medicare Pales Against Health Care Abroad," Richard Eisenberg, nextavenue website, last updated November 15, 2017, http://www.nextavenue.org/medicare-pales-health-care-abroad/.

Are you the kind of person suited for life in a foreign country? Life abroad can be a challenge as well as a pleasure. Consider some of the following questions before you dive headlong into your search for the perfect place to retire on thirty-five dollars a day.

How flexible are you? Utilities and services are not as reliable in many other parts of the world as they are in the United States. How do you react to things you cannot control? Is a forty-eight-hour electricity outage an unfortunate inconvenience for you or a major catastrophe? If the repairperson who told you he would "see you in the morning" to fix your malfunctioning gas stove top doesn't show up by 5:00 p.m., do you shrug, fix a sandwich, and enjoy the rest of your evening, or do you try to reach him by phone every thirty minutes from 2:00 p.m. to 11:00 p.m.? If you chose the latter options, you are probably not suited to life in a more laid-back country like Mexico or Costa Rica.

How close are your family ties and obligations? Are your parents still living? Will they need you to be nearby as they get older? Traveling during major holiday periods or on the spur of the moment during an emergency can be expensive and fraught with delays in the winter months. These are all important considerations. If your family counts on you to be with them for special occasions and emergencies, you will need to find a spot easily accessible by air.

How do you feel about being a "minority"? When you relocate abroad, your face, your language, and your customs will be the exception, not the rule. How do you think you will respond? People may be kind and helpful, but they are not going to learn a new language to converse with you. You are the one who will need to change. You must also be willing to learn new ways of behaving and find new opportunities to connect with people. You may have other Americans around for support, but they won't be your whole world. Transacting business and communicating with health care providers will become an everyday challenge and will shine a spotlight on ways in which your adopted country does things differently than what you are accustomed to. If you approach such differences as being inferior to what you know, you will set yourself up for an extremely disappointing experience.

What are you willing to sacrifice? Living abroad will entail many changes. You may not be able to get your favorite breakfast cereal, your favorite TV programs, or your favorite underwear brand. You will have to make do with what the locals purchase—or pay a lot of money in shipping costs. You may be able to relocate to a college town with rich theater and film offerings, but they will generally not be in English. Nor will the classes themselves, should you wish to learn something new. How attached are you to air conditioning, quiet plumbing, and deli-counter take-out? Take a hard look at all you may have to give up to live in a foreign land.

The questions above are a good self-test for your readiness and suitability for living abroad. The expatriate life can be a wonderful experience, especially for those who do not have strong familial ties to the United States, but do heed the cautionary notes, and above all do your homework. Spend sufficient time in your future home to get a good feel for everyday life. Go at different times of the year. Don't cut all your ties until you're sure life in a foreign country is right for you.

Evaluating Criteria for Living Outside the US

> **If you are considering moving to another country, use this checklist to evaluate the *importance* of the following criteria:**

Safety—how safe do you generally feel in your environment? Are you compulsive about locking doors? Do you carry pepper spray or another defense weapon with you? Are you nervous being out alone at night?

1   2   3   4   5   6   7   8   9   10

Not at all important   Extremely important

Politics—How comfortable are you with other rules of government and law? Are you comfortable with a socialist or communist government? How about a dictatorship?

1   2   3   4   5   6   7   8   9   10

Not at all important   Extremely important

Attitude Toward Americans—Would you be comfortable overcoming negative attitudes about who you are and where you come from?

1   2   3   4   5   6   7   8   9   10

Not at all important   Extremely important

Likelihood of Natural Disasters—Have you had experience living with the likelihood of hurricanes, tornadoes, floods, earthquakes, or volcanic eruptions? Are you comfortable with the likelihood of one or more of these?

1   10

Not at all   2   3   4   5   6   7   8   9   Extremely
important   important

Health Care—How healthy are you currently? Do you need constant monitoring for a health condition? How attached are you to your current doctors?

1   10

Not at all   2   3   4   5   6   7   8   9   Extremely
important   important

Language/Communication—Do you speak another language well enough to converse about important issues? How willing are you to learn another language? Are you willing to take classes to learn another language?

1   10

Not at all   2   3   4   5   6   7   8   9   Extremely
important   important

Ease of Travel—Do you want or need to travel back to the United States frequently? How easily do you travel?

1   10

Not at all   2   3   4   5   6   7   8   9   Extremely
important   important

Entertainment & The Arts—How important to you is American TV, opera, symphony, museums, and theater? Are you willing to give up the kind of entertainment you are used to?

1   10

Not at all   2   3   4   5   6   7   8   9   Extremely
important   important

Shopping—How important is the ability to shop in places like Nordstrom or Target? Will you have trouble giving up the opportunity to buy what you want easily and quickly?

1   2   3   4   5   6   7   8   9   10

Not at all important   Extremely important

Infrastructure and Technology—How attached are you to 24/7 electricity? Fast Internet speeds? Uninterrupted phone service? Will you need these for work?

1   2   3   4   5   6   7   8   9   10

Not at all important   Extremely important

There is an impressive array of options for where you might live in your later years, both within the US and in other countries. If you are intrigued and want to search out more ideas, here are three good places to start:

- TopRetirements.com has an assessment tool called "Retirement Ranger" for finding your ideal spot. It's free when you register on the site. The tool will ask you a series of questions and then email you a report with suggested towns or retirement communities. Each suggestion comes with a link so you can instantly find out more about the destination.

- Ideal-living.com is similar to Top Retirements in that it has a tool for helping you locate retirement communities that would appeal to you, based on a lengthy list of amenities that you can check off. Ideal-living targets retirement communities in the Southeast and Southwest. Once you have done the research, Ideal-living helps you go one step further. They help you book a "discovery tour" so you can take the next step in identifying a retirement community that is right for you.

- Best Cities for Successful Aging (successfulaging.milkeninstitute. org) identifies, measures, compares, and ranks 352 metropolitan areas in the United States on how well they enable older adults to live healthy, independent lives.

As you saw in the contrasting stories of Katie and Tess in Chapter 12, vetting your top choices is critical. You can do that in a number of ways.

- Rent an apartment there for a few months

- Make it your vacation spot for the next several years; visit in all seasons

- Do a home exchange for a month; do it again in a different season

- Subscribe to the local paper for six months to a year

- Find some online communities based where you want to move and chat online with people about their town

Chapter 17. Aging in Place

"He is happiest, be he king or peasant, who finds peace in his home."
—Johann Wolfgang von Goethe

I f moving doesn't appeal to you and you have decided to stay in your current home, then you are among the many older adults who have decided to *age in place*—you want to find a way to remain in your home, on your own, as long as you possibly can. Your success in doing that will depend a lot on how your home is designed and where it is located.

About 87 percent of adults age sixty-five and over want to stay in their current home and community as they age. Among people age fifty to sixty-four, 71 percent of people want to age in a different place.

—Source: AARP 2014 Study

Having chosen to stay put, take a look at the condition of your community. How "livable" is it? A truly livable community takes into consideration the needs of residents of all ages and abilities. A livable community permits everyone to participate in the community-building process and allows its citizens to have independent and meaningful lives. Take a look around you. Can people from a wide variety of socioeconomic levels afford housing? Are there transportation options for all ages? Are the streets safe for walking and biking as well as automobiles? Do all residents have access to healthy food options? Are there support services for those who are unable to access public transportation? Do all residents have access to health care? The AARP Policy Institute has put together a livability index that will allow you to evaluate your community in seven categories and assess the preparations your city or town has made to be a satisfactory home to people of all ages. The AARP index will help you evaluate your community in seven categories:

- Housing – accessibility, options, affordability

- Neighborhood – proximity of jobs, stores, and services; proximity to transit; personal safety, vacancy rate

- Transportation – options, frequency, congestion, convenience, safety, accessibility

- Environment – water quality, air quality, pollution exposure

- Health – access to care, quality of care, prevalence of unhealthy behaviors (e.g., smoking)

- Engagement – Internet access and cost, civic engagement, social engagement

- Opportunity – equality of income, economic advancement, education, age diversity

These categories further break down into over sixty discrete measures. The index is a terrific way to ensure you are staying in (or moving into) a city with policies and a track record of activities that will support you as you age. You will need to do some sleuthing on your own to use the index effectively, but it's worth the effort to know where your community stands on the things that will be important to you in coming years. You will find the index at livabilityindex.aarp.org. You may also want to consider joining a local "village."

The Village Movement

If you decide to age in place, check to see if there is a "village" that covers the area in which you live. The village concept allows people to continue to live in the homes and communities they know and love, with the assistance of a membership-based organization that links together people living within a defined area. It might encompass just one zip code or it may cover an entire county. Members pay a fee, which varies from village to village, but generally, the range is four hundred to twelve hundred dollars a year. This gives them access to a concierge-like service that coordinates and connects them with transportation, help with yard work, basic housecleaning, and prepared meals. Some villages also offer a daily check-in service. In addition, members have access to a list of vetted and discounted services to help them keep their homes safe and in good repair. In many villages these services can be arranged with one phone call to a central office or concierge. Most villages incorporate as a nonprofit, and may employ one or two people to administer and manage the operation. However, members are also expected to volunteer their time and expertise as they are able.

The original village was in the Boston neighborhood of Beacon Hill and was inaugurated in 2001. Although the Beacon Hill Village encompassed a relatively affluent community, models for more modest cities and suburbs are now being developed, relying more on volunteer help to keep the cost as low as possible. As of early 2018, there were over two hundred open villages in the United States, with approximately one hundred fifty more in the formative stages.

The objective of a village is to provide as many services as possible to help people manage on their own and get out into their communities. Because isolation is the greatest danger to aging in place, the village model encourages members to socialize and enjoy the activities they know and love, from live theater and movies to athletic events and nature. Through the screening of service providers, it also reduces the incidence of elder abuse.

Corinne belongs to Avenidas Village in Palo Alto, California, part of the Village to Village Network, and one of the older villages in the United States. Corinne, at age seventy-two, has belonged to Avenidas Village for eight years. She and her husband, Al, joined Avenidas a year and a half before he died, when Al was already quite ill from a neurodegenerative disease.

Because she was caring for Al on a full-time basis, Corinne didn't get involved right away with the social activities Avenidas offered. However, when Al needed to be hospitalized, Corinne reached out to the Avenidas Village volunteer network. The volunteers served as advocates for Corinne and Al in the hospital—taking notes, asking questions, and helping her understand what was happening.

A few months after Al died, Corinne again reached out to Avenidas Village, this time for social connections. She started attending more functions. She joined the "lunch bunch," going to restaurants in the area and enjoying conversations with other members, both men and women.

Avenidas Village also presented Corinne with volunteer opportunities. She joined the advisory council for a few years and became a "cluster leader," organizing activities in her neighborhood and coordinating the ride services that are vital to aging in place. Corinne continues to volunteer for Avenidas on a regular basis, and takes advantage of the many lectures, symphony, opera, and theater trips they offer. She has also found valuable computer assistance when technology takes another leap and threatens to overwhelm her. Corinne has no family in California and realizes she will eventually need to find an alternative to aging in her two-story house. But for now, Avenidas allows her to enjoy her home and her community in a safer and more secure way.

AARP's research on peoples' preferences for where to live as they get older revealed 86 percent of those over forty-five want to stay in their own homes as long as possible. Belonging to a village facilitates and extends independence by five to ten years.

To search the Village to Village Network for a village near you, visit their website: vtvnetwork.org. However, even if you don't have an official "village" in your town, rest assured similar concepts exist around the United States. "The Umbrella" in the Albany/Schenectady area of New York is one such program. (theumbrella.org). The Umbrella is not part of the Village to Village Network, but is similar in its design and mission. In many areas, programs for seniors are often combined with transportation and support services for disabled children and adults under the auspices of a larger city or county program. If you are determined to age in place, I encourage you to find out what exists in your community before you need help. Charles, in the following story, got help just in time from a similar organization:

Charles belongs to a neighborhood organization on Long Island, in New York. They call themselves Neighbors Involved with Neighbors— NIN for short. They are not part of the Village Network, and unlike Avenidas Village and Beacon Hill, NIN does not have any paid staff. However, they have over three hundred members and they operate in much the same way as a village on an all-volunteer basis. Charles hopes to be part of NIN's volunteer corps in the future; for now he pays his dues to use the services, but is unable to give back.

In his youth, Charles was a drinker, a smoker, and a drug user, and though he eventually kicked all three habits, he became a compulsive eater and ballooned up to 443 pounds. A friend recommended he join Overeaters Anonymous (OA), and through OA he was able to begin losing some of the weight that had kept him from walking, driving, or properly caring for himself. Charles was morbidly obese and very close to dying.

After a few months in OA, one of the other members suggested he check out NIN to get some help with his transportation needs. Charles made the call to their hotline and the volunteer on the other end of the phone arranged for Charles to attend a members meeting. That was two years ago. Since then, NIN volunteer drivers have been driving Charles to his doctor appointments, shopping, OA meetings, and the pharmacy. With the help of NIN and OA, Charles has lost 177 pounds and considers NIN volunteers an important part of his "wellness team." Charles lives on a small Social Security check and food stamps. He has no family he can call upon, and relies solely on his NIN connection. He goes to the social gatherings when he feels up to it, and looks forward to getting slimmer, healthier, and regaining his driver's license so he can give back by being a NIN driver for others.

To find out if a village or a program like NIN is available in your area, contact your local Area Agency on Aging. They will know if any such program exists near you.

NORCs (Naturally Occurring Retirement Communities)

A NORC is another way to age in place. A NORC might be a neighborhood, condominium complex, apartment house, mobile home park, or any aggregate of homes where a large percentage of residents happen to be over sixty. They can occur spontaneously anywhere in the world. When NORCs occur in a more affluent area, residents often collaborate and adopt the "village" concept and initiate a membership model with dues and some paid services. When less affluent residents find themselves living in a NORC, their source of support and help generally comes from the local community, each other, senior centers, and services offered by the local Area Agency on Aging.

One of the best examples of a NORC I have ever encountered is a neighborhood in Brenham, a small town about an hour outside of Houston, Texas. Francine, the eighty-five-year-old mother of a friend of mine, lives there and she described it to me this way:

"We are a tiny little no-name neighborhood of about twenty homes, ten of which are owned by people who have been connected to one another in various ways for sixty years and more. Some of us go back to our college days. After college we all dispersed to large ranches and suburbs to raise our families. We stayed in touch. Then one-by-one we left those large homes and ranches and looked for a place to settle in for our older years.

"It all started when one couple we knew discovered Brenham. Then, like dominoes, over the next ten years, we all found our way here. Now we account for half of the little patio home development on this one long block. We like the patio homes. They require far less upkeep than most traditional houses. We have a homeowners' association and the dues take care of the maintenance of the yards, roof repairs, painting—most of the larger tasks we can't manage anymore.

"We aren't all healthy anymore. Cancer has hit one couple very hard. They both have to go to Houston for radiation or chemotherapy treatments. We take turns driving them there. The wife of another couple has advanced Parkinson's. For them we coordinate a "share-the-care" routine, calling to see what they might need, offering rides, lunches, and respite for the husband.

"Everyone on the street is retired, even the ones we didn't know from our younger days. The age range is mid-fifties to upper nineties. Benham is too small to have much industry, so people don't come here to work; they come to retire. All the basics are here: we have a hospital, a senior center, a library, and several event centers. We all know one another and watch out for one another. Some of us belong to the same church. We go to the same clubs, and most of us go to the senior center in town for dances and game nights. We go out together in groups—to movies and to dinner. And almost everyone has a dog."

Francine's experience in her tiny development in Brenham is repeated in hundreds of small towns all over the country. Older condominiums and apartment houses in large cities can also become NORCs. The more proactive the community—in building support systems like "share-the-care," by involving local agencies, and by taking advantage of senior centers and transportation systems—the better they will be able to help one another thrive as they age together.

NORCs are, by definition, grassroots efforts. They require individuals to speak up and take action by developing relationships with relevant agencies to access health care and other public support services, including transportation services, social activities, and in-home repair and maintenance. For more information on NORCs, the best place to start is the website norcblueprint.org.

Many creative ideas for building communities are coming out of the life experiences of baby boomers. Denise's story illustrates a more deliberate form of a NORC. She and her two sisters, none of whom have children, are taking charge of their future in a unique way:

Denise, a high-powered biotech executive in Southern California, is a scientist by training. However, her leadership qualities are what set her apart from her colleagues in the scientific community. Denise's potential as a leader was apparent to her superiors early in her career. Within twelve years of accepting her first job with a large pharmaceutical firm, Denise was asked to head her division. Five years later she took on the role of president of the company's West Coast subsidiary, with over eight hundred employees.

Marriage and children was never part of Denise's plan. That sentiment must run in the family because Denise has two never-married sisters who also have advanced degrees, satisfying careers, and no partners or children. Denise and her sisters are close in age. The middle sister, Candace, is a doctor; the youngest, Erin, is a botanist. Erin had developed a thriving nursery business, but a few years ago she was diagnosed, at age fifty-four, with early-onset dementia. When Erin could no longer run the nursery, her family helped her sell the business. She now does less demanding work as she is able.

Upon Erin's dementia diagnosis, Denise and Candace realized they were all arriving at an age where they needed to think more strategically about the future. Candace gave up her prestigious position at a Seattle area teaching hospital and moved back to Southern California, where she secured a similar position. The entire family, including the sisters' eighty-five-year-old parents, now lived close to one another and they were able to support the youngest sister as she became less able to manage on her own.

Denise and Candace knew the sisters needed to form their own support system as they aged, so they decided to purchase at least two more units in Denise's townhome complex. All three sisters would then live close to one another and would be able to support each other as the need arose. Their plan includes purchasing an additional unit for a caregiver. As of this writing, they have purchased one additional unit, where Erin now lives. Denise has hired a part-time caregiver for Erin—someone to be available when Denise travels. When the next unit in the complex goes on the market, they plan to grab it as well. Denise and her sisters are forming their own support system, and who knows? Others in the complex may want to join them, thereby extending the circle of caring beyond Denise's immediate family.

Home Modifications

If you are determined to stay in your current home as long as you can—alone, with a spouse, or with companions—I urge you to make some physical modifications to your home *before* you need them. Many alterations are simple, while others can be more complex and require a significant outlay of funds. Most are aimed at preventing falls or other injuries, while a newer crop of ideas includes technology to better connect you to the outside world and community resources.

If you are still healthy and strong, planning for aging and possible long-term care can be a puzzle, because you have no way of knowing what you will need. The following chart is based on a 2009 US Department of Health and Human Services Administration on Aging study.

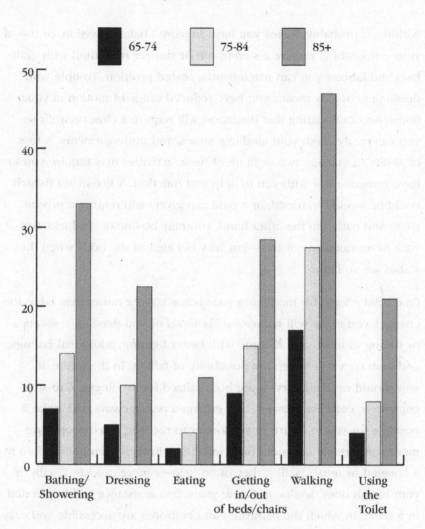

Percent of Persons with Limitations in Activities of Daily Living
by Age Group: 2009

As the chart reveals, relatively few people need help with any of the ADLs (activities of daily living) when they are between the ages of sixty-five and seventy-four. However, at age eighty-five, you stand a good chance of needing help with walking, which means you may require a mobility aid or wheelchair. Those require wider doorways and lower cupboards reachable from a seated position. If you have difficulty bathing, it probably means you have impaired balance, vision, or use of your arms, which require a step-in tub or shower retrofitted with grab bars and faucets you can reach from a seated position. Trouble with dressing generally means you have reduced range of motion in your limbs. Accommodating that limitation will require a closet retrofit so you can easily reach your clothing, shoes, and undergarments. A loss of ability to manage two or more of these activities may require you to have someone live with you to help you function. A live-in aid (which could be a relative, friend, or a paid caregiver) will require a private room and bath. On the other hand, you may be one of the lucky few who never need any of this—but why bet against the odds when the stakes are so high?

One solid reason for modifying your home sooner rather than later: the changes you make will *reduce the likelihood* of you needing assistance or having to move out. A home with better lighting, additional railings, and grab bars will lessen the possibility of falling. In the future, if you should need surgery or are hospitalized for an illness, zero-step entryways, curbless showers, and enlarged passageways will make it possible for you to return home sooner to recover. Since people are more comfortable and safer from infections in their own homes than in a hospital or rehab facility, they often recover more quickly. Finally, if your health does decline in future years, less assistance will be needed in a home in which the bathroom and bedroom are accessible and easy to maneuver in.

Maggie and Ron, both fifty-eight, live in a rural community in upstate New York. They moved there from Brooklyn three years ago after Ron sold his software business. Maggie is a marriage and family therapist who restarted her practice in their rural community after the move. Although Maggie found it emotionally difficult to close down a practice that had been thriving for over twenty years, they both wanted a slower pace of life and a healthier lifestyle.

222

They sold their townhome in Brooklyn and almost immediately found and fell in love with a 1920s farmhouse on thirteen acres. Ron planned to farm the land and Maggie was excited to rebuild her practice in the small, rural community, near where several of her city-fleeing friends had already moved.

The same week they closed escrow on the farmhouse, Ron was diagnosed with multiple sclerosis (MS), a disease that attacks the central nervous system. They learned it is impossible to predict how rapidly the disease will progress, but they knew it would eventually be difficult for Ron to control his balance and muscle coordination. Clearly, spending the rest of his life in a three-story farmhouse was not going to be practical for them.

Maggie researched how homes can be built or modified to accommodate a variety of disabilities and limitations and discovered Universal Design principles. She then contacted an architect who specialized in building homes with these concepts in mind. By the end of that year, they had a plan for a total remodel of the farmhouse to make it suitable for any disability that might arise—for either of them. The plan involved removing the top two stories of the home and adding several rooms onto the main level, such that no stairs were necessary to reach any part of the house.

Today, Maggie and Ron live in a beautiful one-story home, which, at first glance, looks like a home for anyone. However, a closer look reveals a kitchen and bathrooms with countertops at a variety of levels, some with open space underneath, allowing a person to either sit or stand while doing food prep or personal care; extra-wide doorways for both internal and external doors; closets with shelves and bars that can be easily reconfigured; a walk-in shower with no stepover; and attractive insets with grab bars at strategic points around the main rooms. Ron is happily growing apples and grapes, with only occasional symptoms of MS at this point, and Maggie is well on her way to another thriving practice.

Maggie and Ron had a wake-up call they would have been foolish not to heed. However, a majority of us will need either minor or major alterations to our homes if we are to age successfully in them. The following are home modifications and enhancements to consider:

Lighting – ensure your home has a well-lit path to maneuver around the house.

- Replace dim light bulbs with brighter ones. Have an electrician install dimmers on the lights so you can adjust the lighting as you require and save on electricity costs.

- Make sure you have a light switch within reach of the bed.

- Install night lights in all bathrooms and in the kitchen.

- Install additional switches for lamps and overhead lighting in more convenient places. Modern remote-control switches reduce the need for extensive rewiring.

Furniture – keep only what you need, and recycle (sell, give away, donate) the rest. As the years have gone by, have you purchased or inherited more furniture than you need? A cluttered home is a dangerous home. Go through your house and tag those pieces that are superfluous to your lifestyle today. If the object has sentimental value, take a picture of it and move on. If it has been in your family for a long time, offer it to a niece, nephew, or some younger person in your family who could use it to furnish their home. If they don't want it, give it to a charity.

Entryways and Doors

- If you have stairs, check the condition of the railings. Railings deteriorate over time because they are exposed to weather in all seasons and to repeated stress from long-term use. If there is any stairway lacking a railing, install one.

- You may also want to evaluate your entryway for more serious modification at a later date if the need arises. If you have stairs, find out what it would take to install a ramp and who might do the work for you. If a ramp cannot be installed, inquire about installing an electric porch lift.

- Replace door knobs with levers.

Bathroom – An uncluttered and well-equipped bathroom will offer you independence and safety as you get older.

- Install grips and grab bars at a comfortable reach from the toilet and tub

- Purchase a foldable tub seat to have on hand

- Replace knob faucet handles with single-lever models

- Replace your old toilet with a more modern version with a taller seat

- Redesign the vanity to allow a chair to roll underneath

- Redesign your shower to be curbless, with a wide entryway for chair access or to allow an additional person to aid you in the shower

- Remodel a ground-floor bathroom to accommodate you and a caregiver

Bedroom

- Add or convert a ground-floor bedroom

- Furnish the room minimally

- Ensure it stays free of clutter

- Install closet bars at various heights

- Ensure you have a bed at the right height for you to easily get in and out

Kitchen – These modifications and enhancements will allow you to prepare meals and dine independently for as long as possible.

- Install counters at varying heights to allow for seated or standing food prep
- Under-counter space should have room for a chair
- Make sure there is good lighting
- Install cupboards with shelves at reachable heights
- Place microwave oven and toaster oven at counter level
- Clear pathway from food prep area to eating area

Entertainment/Living Area

- Ensure sofas and chairs are at the right height for easy entry and exit
- Remove unnecessary furniture and clutter
- Make sure there is good lighting

Outdoors – access to and enjoyment of the back and/or front yard

- Create no-step access to the yard, patio, or verandah. Install railings by any stairs that cannot be avoided
- Ensure access to both sun and shade
- Install comfortable, easy-access chairs and/or a chaise for relaxing and reading
- Have raised beds built for gardening, if desired
- Install a seated-level potting bench, if desired
- Install motion-triggered lights

Miscellaneous

- Move washer and dryer to the main level of the house (if they are currently in the basement or garage)

- Install slip-resistant flooring in kitchen and bath

- Bare floors are best for mobility devices. Consider removing carpeting and replacing with hard flooring

- Remove throw rugs

Bear in mind a home needs regular cleaning and maintenance. Whether you live in a freestanding house, a condominium, an apartment, or a mobile home/trailer, you will need to make modifications for your home to remain a safe and secure place to age independently. In addition to regular housekeeping, you will need to budget for most or all of the following:

- Your furnace should be inspected annually and filters replaced twice a year

- Gutters need to be cleaned and re-sealed

- Yards need to be mowed, swept, weeded, mulched, etc. on a regular basis

- Snow needs to be removed

- Homes need new roofs every fifteen to twenty years and repainting every ten years or so, depending on siding material and climate

For a person without nearby family, aging in place can be isolating and lonely. Ensuring you have a community and social support will be important. If you intend to age in your home, I urge you to at least have a fallback plan in the event an emergency makes that impossible. In order to create an alternate living plan, you will need to take seriously the information in Chapter 21, "Options for Receiving Care." Do some research in your area. Take a good look at the alternative living options near you, even though you may never need to use them.

If you are planning to age in place, use the following checklist to evaluate your current home for its age-friendliness. You may also find it helpful when you start planning your modifications.

Checklist for an Age-friendly Home[28]

Checkpoint	Yes	No	What I plan to do	Resources I need (people, tools, material)
A step-free entrance				
Lever-style door handles on all entry doors				
Exterior doors at least 36" wide				
Ground-floor bedroom				
Ground-floor bathroom				
Ground-floor kitchen				
Well-lit rooms				
Well-lit hallways				
Dark-activated nightlights in kitchen and bath				
Light switches at top and bottom of stairs				
Throw rugs securely affixed to floor or discarded				
Carpeting in good condition and secure on stairs				
Flooring free of tripping hazards				

28   Adapted from the AARP "Is My Home HomeFit?" checklist, available at http://www.aarp.org/content/dam/aarp/livable-communities/documents-2015/HomeFit2015/01%20Is%20My%20Home%20HomeFit.pdf.

Checkpoint	Yes	No	What I plan to do	Resources I need (people, tools, material)
Handrails on both sides of stairs				
Kitchen cabinets easy to reach				
Lever-style faucets in kitchen				
Kitchen workspace at seated height				
Kitchen appliances reachable from seated position				
Microwave oven and toaster oven at counter level				
Grab bars by toilet and tub/shower				
Exterior walkways well-lit				
Interior doors at least 36" wide				
Shower with a step-free entry or step-in tub				
Lever-style faucets in bathroom(s)				
Non-slip mats in bathtub and/or shower				
Bathroom cabinets easy to reach				
Clutter removed from all rooms				
Electrical cords tucked away and not a tripping hazard				

Checkpoint	Yes	No	What I plan to do	Resources I need (people, tools, material)
Security chain on entry door				
Peep hole or other technology to see who is at your door				
Fire extinguisher within reach of stove and oven				
Home address clearly visible from street				
Smoke and carbon monoxide detectors in every room				
Flashlights in every room				
Bathroom sink and cabinetry that allow seated use				
Washer and dryer at main floor level				

PART IV

ENSURING COMFORT AND CARE IN YOUR OLDEST AGE

Chapter 18. The Trajectory of Aging

"Old age is not for sissies!"

—Malcolm Forbes

Look around you. If you are in your fifties or sixties, you and/or many of your friends are likely spending time and resources providing or ensuring care for your elderly parents. Why now? They took care of themselves up to this time, didn't they? They raised you, didn't they? They had previously made all manner of decisions for themselves. What happened?

Senescence happened. It happens to everyone. In fact, in less obvious ways senescence starts happening when we are in our late twenties. Senescence is the process of aging, the gradual evolution and decline of our bodies and minds. For the most part, we accept these changes as inevitable. We are amazed when pro football quarterbacks are still playing in their late thirties or runners are still doing six-minute miles in their forties.

At forty, you probably couldn't bench press your weight anymore (if you ever could!). Gradually, our muscles begin to lose girth, our skin starts to lose elasticity, and our joints begin to lose cartilage. Most people don't notice this decline until their late forties and early fifties, at which time the changes become more obvious.

Our minds experience senescence too. Mental senescence is less obvious because we compensate as we gain experience. If our minds are at their sharpest when we are in our twenties, why don't we want twenty-five-year-olds running our government or our large corporations? Because they lack experience. Somewhere in our late forties or early fifties, our mental powers couple optimally with our experience base and we are at our peak performance as thought leaders and decision makers.

As we get into our late fifties and sixties, we begin to notice a shift in our mental capacities. We first experience this as a memory issue. Where did I put those car keys? What was that movie I saw the other night? Why did I walk into this room? This can be somewhat scary, and many people question whether or not these experiences are the beginning of dementia. In a small percentage of cases it might be, but more often those memory lapses are simply the natural decline of brain function. In fact, finding a sixty-something person who is *not* experiencing these inconvenience-level memory concerns is rare! Happily, this mental shift also brings some positive changes. As we age we are able to solve problems in a much more holistic way, taking into account the experiences of a lifetime. We become more patient with others and ourselves, and are much more likely to see the issues confronting us in shades of gray, rather than black and white.

How do we prepare today for an uncertain tomorrow?

In our eighties and nineties, we almost always face more life-limiting challenges—like the ones you and your friends are seeing in your aging parents today. The big question is "How do we prepare today for an uncertain tomorrow?" With no adult children around to serve as a safety net underneath us, the sensible path for us is to make some decisions today while our bodies are still functioning adequately and our brains are still relatively sharp.

After the age of eighty-five, the likelihood of needing assistance with one or more ADLs (activities of daily living) increases dramatically. In a 2009 study by the Institute on Aging, 40 percent of men and 53 percent of women age eighty-five or over reported needing help with at least one ADL.[29] Understanding ADLs is important as you contemplate where you might live and what you are likely to need in your oldest days. ADLs are basic self-care tasks essential to maintaining grooming standards and good health. As these tasks become more difficult or impossible for an older person to perform due to lack of mobility, strength, balance, or other physical or mental infirmities, additional aid (long-term care) becomes necessary.

The US Department of Health and Human Services lists the activities of daily living as follows:

- Bathing

- Dressing

- Eating

- Using the toilet

- Transferring (to or from bed or chair)

- Caring for incontinence

In addition, older people often need another level of assistance, sometimes called instrumental activities of daily living (IADLs). They include:

- Housework

- Managing money

- Taking medication

- Preparing and cleaning up after meals

- Shopping for groceries or clothes

- Using the telephone or other communication devices

29   "Read how IOA views aging in America," Institute on Aging, http://www. ioaging.org/aging-in-america.

- Caring for pets

- Responding to emergency alerts such as fire alarms

These ADLs and IADLs are the functions that, for many, become more and more challenging as we age, and they are the reason for the existence of structured communities with trained staff to help with these functions and responsibilities as you lose the ability to perform them yourself. Yes, we all know someone in their nineties who still lives alone without apparent difficulty, and we all want to follow in his or her footsteps. But they are the *outliers*, not the norm.

237

CHAPTER 19. WHAT WILL WE NEED?

"It wasn't raining when Noah built the ark."
—Author unknown

The following are stories of aging *parents*. They are stories of adult children who stepped in to help when the need arose. They provide a snapshot of an average person's final years or months, and give us a window into what those of us without children will need when that time comes.

Muriel and Rex, both in their late nineties, died within four months of each other. The previous five years had been tumultuous. Muriel's painful arthritis had relegated her to life in a wheelchair. In addition, she sometimes got confused about where she was living and who was with her. Rex could still walk, but had significant hearing loss and difficulty maneuvering Muriel's chair from place to place. Rex had given up driving in his early nineties; Muriel had done the same ten years before.

They had five children, nine grandchildren, and seventeen great-grandchildren, most living within a hundred-mile radius. The family had always been close and they saw them frequently at birthday and holiday gatherings. However, none of them had a house suitable for home care for Muriel and Rex. They all wanted the best possible environment for their elders, and determined that assisted living, with specially trained staff, would be the safest and most stable place. After several months of research and visits, they chose a large assisted living facility, not far from two of the daughters.

The family moved Muriel and Rex into their new suite over a long weekend. The couple seemed happy with their new home at first, but the constant changeover of staff left them confused about who they could rely on for what. The confusion led to disorientation. When the children and grandchildren visited they could tell something was wrong; Rex and Muriel were clearly unhappy.

The family decided to try to find a more suitable place. Their search led them to BethsHome, a small board and care facility, located in a converted private home. Luckily, they had a couples' suite available and after a thorough vetting process, the family transferred Muriel and Rex once again. BethsHome suited them better than the less-personal assisted living facility. The owner, Beth, was almost always on the premises and she had trained her staff well. They were caring and consistent. Both Rex and Muriel settled in and each formed a strong attachment to one special staff member.

Muriel's and Rex's world eventually shrank to include only each other, the staff at BethsHome, and the regular visits from children and grandchildren. The children picked up prescriptions from the pharmacy, brought in special foods they liked, and made sure their parents had adequate clothing and footwear for the season. Although the staff at BethsHome were excellent at their jobs, caring and patient with both Muriel and Rex, the children oversaw every aspect of their care and were vigilant in making sure their parents were happy and lacked for nothing.

In June, when Muriel contracted a bacterial infection that ultimately took her life, Rex began to change. He seemed to be increasingly out of touch with the world around him and began to live more in his inner world. The visits from children and grandchildren continued, with a greater focus on simply being there with him. Finally, in November, a short-lived bout of pneumonia claimed his life as well.

Pat died at home at age ninety. Over the course of her life she had carefully managed a tricky liver condition and a digestive abnormality. Eventually the liver condition overwhelmed her body's defenses and exhausted the ability of medical science to keep it under control. Pat knew she was nearing the end of her life and didn't want to spend her final days in a hospital. Her husband and her adult children made it possible for her to remain at home as the liver failure continued to weaken her constitution.

Over a six-month period, her family turned an office into a ground-floor bedroom and made special meals that she could tolerate. Pat's husband Andrew, much luckier in health, played a major role in Pat's care, and her adult children and grandchildren were frequently around to lend a hand and provide company to Pat as she lived out her days. They stayed with Pat while Andrew went for a round of golf or lunch with friends—a needed respite for any caregiver. Pat died in her own bed with her husband, her daughter, her son, and their spouses at her side.

The stories of Muriel, Rex, and Pat are stories of aging *parents*. This is how thoughtful, loving families treat their elders. Some stories aren't quite as pretty, of course, because some people aren't as caring or close to their families. But you and I and the rest of the fifteen million people without children in the boomer generation will need to write our own stories—ahead of time. We will need to figure out how and where we want to spend the rest of our lives and our final days—the phase of life some experts now call "deep aging."

Government research reveals that a sixty-five-year-old today has around a 70 percent chance of developing a mental or physical condition, for a period of at least three months, that will limit their ability to perform two or more of the critical tasks of daily living.[30] Sometimes these events are temporary setbacks, and the ability for self-care and conscious decision-making returns. Sometimes the condition lasts for the rest of life. If that happens to you and you are not in a position to make your own medical decisions, you will need someone to make them for you. Wouldn't *you* rather decide who that person will be and ensure that they understand what *you* want?

Long-Term Care

Today, most of us hear the term "long-term care" in the context of insurance. However, whether or not you decide to purchase long-term care insurance, understanding the true meaning of long-term care is essential. A common misperception is that Medicare covers long-term care. It DOES NOT. Why not? Because long-term care is not "medical" in nature. Long-term care includes a wide range of services and support designed to help older and disabled people with routine personal care—those ADLs and IADLs covered in Chapter 18.

The statistics on disability and the need for some kind of long-term care are tough to hear, but we must understand and acknowledge them. Seventy percent of people who reach the age of sixty-five can expect to use some form of long-term care during their lives.[31] Will these statistics include you? No one knows. People of any age may temporarily or permanently lose the ability to care for themselves, but the odds go up dramatically as we get older.

---

30   "How Much Care Will You Need?," last modified October 10, 2017, US Department of Health and Human Services Website, *https://longtermcare.acl.gov/the-basics/how-much-care-will-you-need.html.*

31   "How Much Care Will You Need?," last modified October 10, 2017, US Department of Health and Human Services Website, *https://longtermcare.acl.gov/the-basics/how-much-care-will-you-need.html.*

In past generations this challenge was contained and managed by the families of those who needed this care. Because few people lived into their eighties and nineties with long-term chronic conditions, long-term care was far less of an issue. The problem was small for society as a whole, so unless your family was caring for an elder or disabled member, you wouldn't have thought or heard much about long-term care. Today, the "big three killers"—heart attacks, strokes, and cancer—are not necessarily killing people. Survivors of these events continue to live, sometimes regaining normal functioning, sometimes needing care for an extended period. Those who are able to resume their lives without needing assistance live on to face the next health crisis. At some point, additional help will be required to meet other medical needs or the activities of daily living.

By the year 2050, the over-eighty-five age group will *triple* as a percentage of the population. That statistic raises another specter we must face: medical science has been tracking and studying the incidence of Alzheimer's and other forms of dementia for several decades now. They estimate close to one-third of those who reach age eighty-five will experience some level of dementia.[32] Will you be among them? No one knows.

The statistics are quite clear. We must take those numbers into consideration as we plan for the best possible quality of life during our later decades. Sorting out your long-term care plan before a crisis hits should be at the top of your "to do" list. Having to sort out how and where you are going to get long-term care at the moment of crisis is stressful—and often ends badly. If you plan ahead when you have the time to think through the options, do the research, and put it in writing, all you or your designated agent have to do is set in motion the plans you made. If you never need it, that's great.

---

32   Alzheimer's Association, "2015 Alzheimer's Disease Facts and Figures" Alzheimer's & Dementia 2015 11(3): 332-84. Available at https://www.alz.org/facts/downloads/facts_figures_2015.pdf.

There are things you can do, of course, to reduce your odds of needing care, or at least postponing your need for it. Continuing to be physically and mentally active will be your best ally in your quest for continued good health and stamina. As little as a twenty-minute daily walk will help keep your joints and your heart in good shape. Learning something new will keep your mind sharp and active. You can do this by working at a job, volunteering, taking a class, joining an interest group or a book club, learning to play a musical instrument, playing bridge or mahjong, or picking up a new hobby (e.g., photography, bird-watching, ballroom dancing, woodworking—anything that requires learning). Socializing and interacting with people will help you stay sharp and maintain good eating and grooming habits.

CHAPTER 20. FINANCING THE CARE YOU NEED

I f you had a need for long-term care tomorrow, where would the money come from and who would provide the care? That is a question we all need to answer in order to feel secure about our future well-being and comfort.

Long-term care expenses may cost more during your lifetime than any other single expenditure. These costs vary by location, the severity of the condition, and the place where you receive the care. Your home might be the *least* expensive or the *most* expensive place to receive care, depending on what you need. Medicare or other insurance generally covers skilled nursing, regardless of whether it is administered in your home or in a skilled nursing facility. However, once medical care is no longer necessary, the need for follow-on help with ADLs and IADLs can be lengthy and expensive.

"The Medicaid system currently steers people toward nursing home care. Far more people can be covered in community-based care programs for significantly less."

—Ed Rendell, former governor of Pennsylvania

In 2012, the national average rate for a non-skilled caregiver to come to your home was $21.00 per hour. Assuming a basic level of care for six hours per day, the total would be $126 per day or $45,990 per year. That would be in addition to your overall cost of living (food, housing, home maintenance, transportation, etc.). The national average monthly base rate in an assisted living community in 2012 was $3550 per month or $42,600 per year. Those rates have continued to climb over the past few years, and you can double that figure if you live in a high-cost urban area. AARP and MetLife both have tables and calculators on their respective websites for determining costs in your area.

There are four ways to pay for long-term care:

1. Personal assets (savings, home equity, etc.)

2. Insurance (long-term care, life, and other insurance hybrids)

3. Medicaid (or the state equivalent, like Medi-Cal in California)

4. Funds from other family members (siblings, nieces, nephews, etc.)

You may be thinking at this point ... "What about Medicare?" No, Medicare *does not* cover long-term care. Nor does a Medicare supplement. None of the Medicare or Medicare-related programs covers long-term care.[33] You can confirm this for yourself on the Medicare website. And now you might be thinking ... "Surely my private health insurance covers long-term care." No, it doesn't. Check your policy. Long-term Care Insurance (LTCI) or an LTC/Life hybrid is the only kind of insurance that covers long-term care. However, LTCI is expensive, and not suitable for everyone.

This information might be scary and depressing. But the alternative, leaving everything to chance, is even scarier, especially for those of us without kids. Planning ahead will educate you and take much of the unknown out of the equation.

---

33   "What Part A & Part B doesn't cover," Medicare.gov website, http://www. medicare.gov/what-medicare-covers/not-covered/item-and-services-not-covered-by-part-a-and-b.html.

Long-Term Care Insurance

Depending on your personal finances and your extended-family situation, you may or may not be a good candidate for long-term care insurance. LTCI can be an important component of planning for people without children, but there are other options if you are not able to afford it or don't qualify for it.

Like life insurance, the younger you are when you purchase LTCI, the less it costs. Consulting with a financial planner will help you determine whether you should make this investment. If they think you are a good candidate for LTCI, they will be able to recommend a knowledgeable, independent LTC insurance broker in your area. If you choose someone who *specializes* in LTC insurance, they will be able to guide you with the current policy options.

Personal Assets

If you have made (and saved) quite a bit of money during your lifetime or have inherited a sizeable sum, you may be in a position to self-finance your long-term care. The actual dollar figure necessary will depend on the area of the country in which you are living—or plan to live. A financial planner and/or elder care attorney can help you make this determination. Even if you have saved some money or stand to inherit some, you may also wish to supplement it with a small amount of LTC insurance. All these options are possible.

Medicaid

The remaining option is Medicaid, a program funded by federal and state money and administered by the state. Each state has a unique set of rules surrounding eligibility for the aid. In most states you will qualify for this type of assistance if you have depleted all your other resources.

Though the federal government has guidelines for the programs, each state interprets them differently. At a basic level, to qualify for Medicaid you must:

- Be a US citizen or a "qualified alien" and a resident of the state where you file your application.

- Demonstrate the need for long-term care, certifying you cannot perform several of the "activities of daily living" (ADLs) necessary for your survival.

- Have less than the allowable dollar value of assets.

- Have income too low to cover the actual cost of your care.

In most states, there are rules in place to protect married couples from impoverishing the spouse who does not need care. These guidelines generally include allowing the spouse to keep the home and a certain amount of income. Nolo Press (nolo.com) has some good information in their books and on their website about how and when Medicaid pays for long-term care in assisted living communities or nursing homes.[34]

Pre-planning for Medicaid makes sense in some situations. Medicaid planning means positioning your income and assets so you can legally qualify for Medicaid if you need it. You may have a negative reaction to this idea, based on stories you have heard about wealthy people

---

34   "When Will Medicaid Pay for a Nursing Home or Assisted Living?," Elizabeth Dickey, nolo.com website, http://www.nolo.com/legal-encyclopedia/when-will-medicaid-pay-nursing-home-assisted-living.html.

milking the Medicaid system by giving away all their assets, but that is rarely the case. Medicaid should be treated as a last-resort solution. My friend Ron recently helped his aunt qualify for Medicaid:

Ron is a financial advisor, not an attorney, but he is well-connected with estate attorneys and got good advice from them as well as from the office of social services in their area. Ron's aunt Sharon was partially estranged from the rest of the family, showing up sporadically for family events and often disappearing from their lives for years at a time. She is an artist by profession, she never married or had kids, and she never made or saved much money. At age sixty-five she was diagnosed with early-onset dementia.

Sharon's dementia developed slowly, and for a few years she remained in her small condominium in downtown Chicago. She didn't know many other people in the building but had friends in the city, so when those friends started to call Ron with concerns about Sharon's erratic thought patterns and behavior, Ron hired a senior care manager to look in on her several times a week. That solution held things together for about a year, but then she lost her car on two occasions and started drinking more heavily. Eventually a concerned neighbor called Adult Protective Services.

At that point Ron got much more involved. He was able, with the help of other family members, to get her to sign an advance health care directive (AHCD) and a power of attorney making Ron the agent for health decisions, finances, and property. The senior care manager told Ron that Sharon was not safe in her condo any longer without someone watching her on an ongoing basis. At that point Ron moved her into a small unit in a private-pay assisted living facility with memory care.

Once Sharon settled into assisted living, Ron sold her condo. The profits from the condo, combined with a very small pension from the days when she taught art, allowed Sharon to live in the memory care facility on independent funds for almost four years. However, Sharon had no long-term care insurance, and by year four her funds had completely run out.

Sharon is now in one of the two rooms available at below-market rates in the memory care facility, and Ron is in the process of proving to the state of Illinois that Sharon's resources have run out. When he has done so, Sharon can go on the Medicaid program in Illinois. Ron is certain he will get her on the program, but being on Medicaid isn't a guarantee Sharon can continue to live in her current memory care facility. Most states still have no provision for Medicaid recipients to be housed where they can receive the assistance with daily living they need. The last resort is moving Sharon to a skilled nursing facility, where she can receive "medical care" (which she doesn't need), the only kind of assistance Medicaid covers.

Ron's story highlights the times we live in. Because the federal Medicaid program is in the hands of the states to administer, it differs from state to state. This kind of situation is one we all want to avoid because the stories you hear about Medicaid recipients getting substandard care compared to private-pay residents are, unfortunately, sometimes true. However, Medicaid planning may be the best option for you if you don't qualify for LTC insurance, can't afford it, or haven't saved enough to cover a long-term care need. You may want to investigate this issue further with an elder law attorney or legal aid.

If you are considering Medicaid planning, you would be wise to do some groundwork and research now. Some assisted living communities and nursing homes don't take Medicaid, while others do. Some allocate a certain number of beds for Medicaid patients, with the rest allocated to private-pay residents. Checking out the rules in your state and the resources in your desired area should be a critical part of your plan. You will most likely find some residential facilities appeal to you more than others. Be sure to run a Better Business Bureau check as well as a licensure bureau inquiry on any facilities that look like good candidates for taking Medicaid recipients.

PLEASE NOTE: The rules on Medicaid and the options for long-term care insurance vary from state to state and change on a yearly basis. I am not a credentialed expert in either of these areas. I strongly encourage you to seek out professional advice before acting on any of the ideas or suggestions mentioned in the stories or narrative in this chapter.

CHAPTER 21. OPTIONS FOR RECEIVING CARE

Let us step into a seaworthy craft
To ply through storms of care
Ride the peaks and troughs
Endure the rains of doubt
Set anchor in the harbor of Hope

Let us be there
And write a new song
For what has been lost
And what gained therefrom
I can do the words, you can hum a tune

—"A Sea Change in Care" by Barbara Greer

This chapter focuses on options for your oldest age. The ideas and suggestions probably won't sound very appealing to you if you are reading this book at age fifty-something or sixty-something, or even seventy-something, but the statistics don't lie. Most of us will need some help as we age. If we want to continue to have control over our lives, we must plan for the future and make some choices while we are still strong and healthy.

A conversation about personal preferences for later-life care can be difficult for many people. When I ask my clients and friends where they want to be when they can no longer care for themselves, I get quite a number of flippant answers. I have heard "Just shoot me," "I'll take the black capsule," and "If that happens, I won't care anyway." Well I can

251

assure you that you will care, and no one is going to hand you a gun! Why not do the research while you can? This chapter will help you better understand the housing choices for later life and decide where you would prefer to receive care, if and when you need it.

Family members frequently provide—either personally or financially—the short-term and long-term care for aging kin who have remained in their own home. Family-provided aid is the most cost-effective way to manage the expense of care, and has the additional appeal of allowing older adults to stay in familiar surroundings. According to an AARP-sponsored survey, "Caregiving in the US 2015,"[35] today's families provide 86 percent of the long-term care for aging kin. Forty-seven percent of that care is provided for a parent or parent-in-law.

Will family care be available to you? Can you imagine moving in with a sibling or niece or nephew and their family—or moving a family member in with you?

If you can answer "yes" to the question above, I encourage you to start the discussion now with these family members, to make sure they concur. Be sure to discuss the nature of the help you might need and what level or intensity they are prepared to provide. They may well be physically and emotionally prepared to help you dress, drive you to appointments and shopping, and would happily share meals with you if you are unable to cook for yourself. But are they ready to help you with more intimate activities, like bathing and toileting? This kind of discussion will probably not be easy, but I recommend having it.

If family aid will not be available or doesn't sound appealing to you, you will want to consider the alternatives. In the past, nursing homes,

35   "Research Report: Caregiving in the U.S. 2015 – Focused Look at Caregivers of Adults Age 50+," *National Alliance for Caregiving (NAC)* website, http://www.caregiving.org/wp-content/uploads/2015/05/2015_CaregivingintheUS_Care-Recipients-Over-50_WEB.pdf. The full report and related materials can be found at http://www.caregiving.org/caregiving2015/.

which are similar to hospitals—institutional settings without much attention to aesthetics or aspects of care other than medical—were the only alternative. Happily, several other options are available today. Designing an alternative care plan and discussing it with your family or friends is important. Why? Because in a crisis, the nearest nursing home will most likely be the default choice if no one in your family knows about other options or what you want. Nursing homes in the United States start at $50,000 per year and can run as high as $250,000 per year, based on the quality of the institution and the state in which you reside.[36] Your stay may be covered by Medicare and private insurance for up to a hundred days after you are discharged from a hospital, but if you don't need medical care beyond that time, the cost will be billed to you. A nursing home will deplete your resources faster than any other option mentioned in this book.

With sufficient financial resources, you can hire whatever level of care you need, from meal drop-off services to full-time nursing care in your own home. Long-term care insurance, if you have it, will cover some or most of the cost. If you don't have the personal resources or a long-term care insurance policy, it's time to think about where you would prefer to live should you need care. Remember, no matter how healthy you are today, the government statistics tell us from age sixty-five onward, we have a 70 percent chance of needing long-term care at some point in later life.[37]

You are probably quite capable now of making sound decisions, avoiding scams on the Internet and mail, and checking out the references of hired aides, etc. However, if you suffer a fall or need surgery in your eighties or nineties and need immediate help in your

---

36   "What Is Covered By Health & Disability Insurance?," LongTermCare.gov website, last modified October 10, 2017, *https://longtermcare.acl.gov/costs-how-to-pay/what-is-covered-by-health-disability-insurance/*.

37   "The Basics," LongTermCare.gov website, last modified October 10, 2017, *https://longtermcare.acl.gov/the-basics/*.

home, how will you arrange and manage those services? If you are determined to stay in your home, I urge you to think now about who you might recruit—a trusted younger family member, a professional fiduciary, an attorney—to manage the vetting of services and the financial part of this plan. And even if you make these arrangements, you will still be opening the door to the possibility of ending up in a nursing home at some point if your designee exhausts all the options at their disposal. Therefore, please give strong consideration to exploring some of the following alternatives to aging in place.

Continuous Care Retirement Community (CCRC)

A CCRC, sometimes called a "life care" community, may be the right answer *if* the cost fits your pocketbook. Offering independent living, assisted living, and skilled nursing, these communities are an excellent option for those that want to be assured of a stable place to live where they will receive whatever care they require until the end of life. CCRCs offer the assurance of being the last home you ever need. However, most CCRCs have a policy that requires new residents to be relatively healthy and able to live independently *when they move in*, and you must be able to demonstrate you are financially capable of continuing to pay your monthly fees, with a cushion for emergencies. Dana chose a CCRC at age sixty-nine:

> Dana comes from a close-knit family in the Midwest. At ten, Dana decided she wanted to be a nurse. Her mother had been a nurse and she loved listening to her stories about helping people overcome illnesses and injuries. She saw how happy her mother became when one of her charges was released from the hospital and got to go home "good as new."

Upon graduation from high school, she looked for the shortest path to her destined career and chose the army. Three years later, Dana found herself on an airplane bound for Vietnam. For the next two years, Dana worked as a nurse in a Mobile Army Surgical Hospital (MASH) just south of Saigon. She loved the challenging, ever-changing work and the close-knit world of a MASH unit. Additionally, the respect and honor bestowed upon her by her patients sustained her through some very tough times as the war drew to its unhappy close.

In the late 1960s, when Dana joined the Army Medical Corps, the rules for enlisting included the stipulation she could not be married or have children throughout the tenure of her service. That didn't pose a problem for Dana because she was, at the time, struggling within herself about her sexual orientation.

Once out of Vietnam, the army kept her moving for the rest of her twenty-six-year career. She enjoyed wonderful experiences in Europe, with easy duty and lots of time for recreation. Still, she relocated too often to form lasting bonds with a romantic partner, so she kept things light, focusing on furthering her education, which the army supported.

By age thirty, Dana knew she was gay, but homosexuality was still illegal in most states and against the regulations for military life, so she kept her sexual orientation a secret, discussing it only with others in the same situation. When she left the army for civilian life, Dana was almost fifty and had met Rita, a college professor. They made a life together in the civilian world. Rita continued to teach and do research, and Dana found opportunities to continue working in the medical field until her mid-sixties when she began to wind down.

When Dana was sixty-nine, she and Rita moved into a CCRC. They had checked out many options in the Chapel Hill, North Carolina, area and chose one with an excellent reputation for health care, as well as a tradition of acceptance of all sexual preferences. From their first visit, management knew of their status as a gay, married couple. They were welcomed warmly, and felt at home almost immediately.

Dana is still involved with her family and speaks fondly of them. A niece and nephew came to her wedding, and her nephew stayed with them to provide extra care when Dana had knee surgery a few years ago. Dana and her brother are close and talk often, but because Dana and Rita do not have children of their own, they realized they had to provide for their future in the best way they could. For them, an open, accepting CCRC presented the ideal option.

The concept of the CCRC evolved from nonprofit religious communities seeking to offer a more attractive alternative to almshouses for those who could contribute something financially to their own care and housing. Lutherans, Baptists, Episcopalians, Quakers, Jews, and others all supported these kinds of communities; some still do. They were well known in the early- to mid-twentieth century, when many religious communities had amassed adequate funds to cover any expenses that went beyond what their resident parishioners could pay. Of course, people didn't live as long as they do today. Even thirty years ago, most residents lived only a few years beyond their move-in date.

Today's CCRCs operate on a tiered system, accommodating residents at whatever level of independence they can safely manage. CCRC services typically include:

- Meals (including special diet accommodations)

- Housekeeping

- Scheduled (and sometimes unscheduled) transportation (to medical appointments, shopping, entertainment)

- Recreational, social, and educational activities on-site and off-site

- Grooming assistance (hairdressing and nail care services)

- Personal assistance

- Assisted living (when and if necessary)

- Skilled nursing (when and if necessary)

Many CCRCs are run as nonprofits, though today a growing number are set up as for-profit businesses and corporations. Regardless of their economic model, most of them offer one or more of the following types of contracts:

1. **Life Care Contracts** involve a hefty entrance or buy-in fee plus a standard monthly fee for any level of care required, with the potential for modest annual fee increases as the cost of labor and materials rises. A life care contract guarantees the facility will provide care, as needed, for the rest of a resident's life, even if their funds run out. These are the most expensive contracts, with high entrance fees, often requiring a transfer of most of the resident's assets.

2. **Modified Contracts** involve a monthly fee with a guarantee of access to higher levels of care. Although the entrance fee and monthly rate starts out lower than with the life care contract, the monthly rate will go up when the resident requires additional care, which is billed on an à la carte basis, usually at lower-than-market rates. In this way, the resident shares the additional risk of future care costs with the provider.

3. **Fee-for-Service Contracts** are similar to the modified contract, guaranteeing higher levels of care when needed, but with little or no discount. The resident assumes all risk for future care costs and generally pays them at market rate.

In most CCRCs, the resident does not purchase the unit as real estate; they buy the right to occupy it until they pass on or move up to a more intensive level of care, often in a different part of the facility. However, there are still a few CCRCs that require the resident to purchase the unit as a real estate transaction. Jim and his wife, Erica, provide a good example of why people choose CCRCs when they can afford it:

Jim and Erica moved into a CCRC near Silicon Valley in California seven years ago when they were both seventy-four. The motivation for their move was twofold. Erica had started to develop some complications of high blood pressure and had to stop driving. At about the same time, Jim, a professional mediator, attended a local conference on aging and learned about different options for senior care. Jim and his wife started researching communities in their area. When they found their spot, they signed a contract, sold their nearby home, and moved in.

Jim and Erica look back at their decision and continue to congratulate themselves for making the move. They love living in their new community. They take long walks every day in the nearby open space preserve. Jim still drives, and they often join old friends for dinner or theater in the nearby town where they used to live. They also do a lot of entertaining, either in their home or in one of the private dining rooms the CCRC makes available to residents for this purpose.

With a CCRC, new residents, who are typically in their mid-seventies to mid-eighties, start out in an independent-living apartment, duplex, or small, single-family home (buy-in costs vary by unit size) and remain there as long as possible. The CCRC contract generally includes one or two meals per day, regardless of the new resident's level of independence upon arrival. When a resident begins to need help with activities of daily living, they receive assistance from the staff, in their own unit or in a separate section of the facility better equipped for assisted living. If they are too ill for assisted living, they are moved into the skilled nursing section of the facility until they are able to live independently again ... or for their final days.

If you decide that a CCRC might be in your future, do your research on any facility you are considering. As with nursing homes, the federal government has left oversight of these facilities to the states, so your first piece of research should be your state's regulations and governance of these kinds of businesses. The California Advocates for Nursing Home Reform (CANHR.org) is an excellent resource, even if you don't reside in California. The downloadable publication "Continuing Care Retirement Communities in California: Is One Right for You?" can be found in the resource section of their website.[38]

Once you find a CCRC that interests you, I suggest you have both an attorney and a financial advisor look over the contract with you. Together you should look at:

- Services the fee covers

- Provisions for fee increases

- Funds (if any) to assist residents who run out of money

- The refund policy (if any)

- Clauses governing voluntary and involuntary discharges

In addition to the contract, you and your professional advisors should inquire into the policies and track record of the organization. What is their history of fee increases? What experience can they claim in operating both independent-living communities (e.g., Hyatt Corp.) and communities administering a higher level of care (e.g., Sunrise Senior Living)? What's the current occupancy rate? What is their current financial condition? How healthy is their reserve fund? They should be willing to open the books to you. Are there any complaints registered with the Better Business Bureau or lawsuits pending by families or former residents? In addition to the CANHR website, in 2013 Kiplinger's published an excellent and thorough article on evaluating and choosing a CCRC.[39]

---

38   "*Continuing Care Retirement Communities in California: Is One Right for You?*," California Advocates for Nursing Home Reform (CANHR), http://www.canhr.org/publications/PDFs/CCRCGuide.pdf.

39   Eleanor Laise, "*Risks and Rewards of Moving to a CCRC,*" Kiplinger, January 1, 2013. Available at http://www.kiplinger.com/article/retirement/T037-C000-S000-

CCRCs are at the top of the food chain for retirement living, meaning they are the most expensive option. However, more modest ones are now opening, especially in the Midwest, the south, and the mid-Atlantic area, so even if you have not put aside a large amount of money for your later years, a CCRC or similar type of community may still be possible for you. Because they change so frequently, I am reluctant to publish fee schedules and buy-in costs. However, to give you an idea of costs in an expensive area, the 2016 buy-in rate for California CCRCs started around $200,000 and went well over a million dollars for the fancier properties. Most people sell their homes and use the accumulated equity for the buy-in. The monthly fees must then come from income sources and reserves (savings and investments). They range from $2,500 per month (at the independent level) to over $8,000 when a resident requires full nursing care, depending on what kind of contract is in place.

If you think a CCRC might be in your future, go beyond your computer research and visit one (or more) of them in your desired area. Talk to the residents as well as the staff, and hang around as long as the staff will let you to get a sense of the place. Do people seem happy? Are they engaged with each other and with the staff? Do you see evidence of positive activity taking place around you? Do the staff members talk respectfully to the residents? Get a "gut feel" for a place in addition to asking the questions.

To find out more about CCRCs in your community, check out the caregiving resource center on AARP's website: AARP.org/home-family/caregiving.

---

risks-and-rewards-of-moving-to-a-ccrc.html.

Assisted Living Communities

Assisted living facilities are well known to those who have had to arrange care for an aging parent in the last twenty years. Today assisted living communities are the fastest growing type of care setting. They meet the needs of many older adults who do not need constant medical care but do need help with some of the activities of daily living (ADLs). However, the concept of assisted living is relatively new—an outgrowth, no doubt, of the increasing numbers of people whose lives are saved by modern medicine but who cannot manage all the requirements of daily living on their own.

ALFA, the Assisted Living Federation of America (now rebranded as "Argentum"; argentum.org), has defined an assisted living residence as a "combination of housing, personalized support services, and health (not *medical*) care, designed to meet the needs—both scheduled and unscheduled—of those who need help with the activities of daily living." Residents in assisted living are typically in their late seventies, eighties, and nineties. Some assisted living communities are licensed for memory care (Alzheimer's disease and other forms of dementia), but others are not. However, memory care is one of the fastest growing needs, and most assisted living communities are in the process of getting trained and licensed to accept residents with this diagnosis.

Many assisted living communities now offer prospective residents the opportunity to move in at an "independent living" level (much like a CCRC), stepping up the level of care when they need it. These communities differ somewhat in the range of services they provide, but the following are typical:

- Housekeeping

- Transportation

- Assistance with eating, bathing, dressing, toileting, and walking

261

- Access to health and medical services

- Memory care (if certified)

- Twenty-four-hour security

- Emergency call systems

- Medication management

- Laundry services

- Social and recreational activities

Assisted living is paid from private funds. Medicare does not cover this level of care because it is not medical. According to the national Cost of Care Survey by Genworth Financial, the 2014 median rate for a one-bedroom unit in an assisted living facility stood at $3,500 per month,[40] which amounts to $42,000 per year. The cost differs from location to location, and as with most residential alternatives, will vary with the value of the land on which it sits, the level of staffing, and the amenities the program provides.

Well over one million Americans live in assisted living communities today. Around the country there are approximately forty thousand such communities. As you begin to explore the assisted living communities in your area, Argentum (formerly ALFA) can provide you with an excellent consumer checklist for evaluating them.[41]

---

40   "Genworth 2014 Cost of Care Survey," Genworth website, https://www. genworth.com/dam/Americas/US/PDFs/Consumer/corporate/130568_032514_ CostofCare_FINAL_nonsecure.pdf

41   The checklist can be found at https://www.argentum.org/wp-content/ uploads/2017/08/Argentum-Guide-to-Choosing-a-Senior-Living-Community.pdf.

Board and Care Homes

These are private dwellings, usually a converted home, where the homeowner along with paid staff provides care for individuals who are in some way disabled or need help with ADLs. Often comparable in cost, well-run board and care homes can be a good alternative for people who need assistance and find the larger, more impersonal, assisted living communities unappealing.

Board and care homes are far less institutional in feel than most assisted living facilities, and can be less expensive. They are *much* less expensive than a nursing home. They provide a safe, supportive environment, though they seldom have medical care available beyond a visiting nurse. Some board and care homes specialize in specific conditions, like Alzheimer's or Parkinson's, if they are licensed to do so. Some may admit only men or only women because of a lack of privacy; others serve a general population of individuals who need assistance. If you are married, inquire whether they are equipped to handle a married couple. If you both eventually need this kind of assistance, you don't want to find out at the eleventh hour that all the rooms have one single bed.

Board and care homes are not regulated by the federal government or most states, although many states have their own licensing requirement. Because of this lack of regulation, checking on their reputation is vital. If you find one suitable for your future needs, ask for references—and *call them*. You will want to talk to a son or daughter of someone who lives or lived there. Ask them how often they visited, whether their parent had any problems there, and how happy they appeared during a visit. You should also check with the state licensing agency for board and care homes to determine if the facility has had complaints. Arriving unannounced for visits at various times of the day will give you a good idea of what is taking place when they don't expect visitors. You will get a snapshot of how the residents look, what they are doing, and how many staff members are on shift at a particular hour of the day.

Board and care homes use a standard contract for services, and you would be well served to ask an attorney to review it with you. Like assisted living communities, board and care homes are paid for with private funds or through long-term care insurance. Medicare does not cover them. Make sure to discuss with them the different methods of paying for the care you would receive.

Even as a child-free, independent sixty-something, you may think it silly to be researching care facilities and interviewing their management when you are still healthy and strong, yet we never know when the need will arise. In addition, there is no guarantee a particular assisted living community or board and care home will have space for you when you need it.

Nursing Homes

According to the CDC, there are over 1.4 million people over sixty-five living in nursing homes today.42 Nursing homes (also called skilled nursing facilities) are familiar to most of us because they have been around longer than any other kind of long-term care residence. You may have had a grandparent who lived in one for an extended period of time. Their generation didn't have choices like assisted living communities or CCRCs.

Nursing homes are a critical link in the continuum of care for the long term. They are the only facilities licensed to provide medical

---

42   L. Harris-Kojetin et al., Long-Term Care Providers and Services Users in the United States: Data from the National Study of Long-Term Care Providers, 2013–2014 (National Center for Health Statistics, Vital Health Stat. 3(38), 2016). Available at https://www.cdc.gov/nchs/data/series/sr_03/sr03_038.pdf.

care and attention on a round-the-clock basis. Some people require that level of care for a long time. Most nursing homes now also serve as "rehabilitation facilities." Along with the elderly residents, you will sometimes see middle aged and even young people there for a short stay after procedures like hip replacements or back surgery. Unfortunately, however, most of the elderly nursing home residents are there for the long-term, even though they may not need that level of care on a continuing basis.

Nursing homes are VERY expensive because they are designed for people who need constant medical care that requires expensive staffing and equipment. People who are frail, have a severe chronic disability, or have advanced dementia rarely need that level of care. They need a safe and supportive place to live and help with some or all of the ADLs. Caring and well-trained aides can perform those tasks in CCRCs, assisted living communities, and board and care homes. Relegating someone to a nursing home when they don't require round-the-clock medical care is like hitting a flea with a sledgehammer—unnecessary and wasteful.

Lack of advance planning and/or lack of funds are the reasons many of today's frail older adults still end up in nursing homes—sometimes for many years. With a doctor's orders, Medicare will cover the cost of nursing home care for a limited period of time, and if there are no other funds available, Medicaid (your state's version) will pick up the tab when Medicare runs out, given certain conditions. Few people need a nursing home's level of care for long, but unfortunately, they have become a default solution for those with limited financial resources.

With good planning, anyone can avoid a nursing home's expensive, long-term confinement. However, especially if you are single, you may still need a place for short-term rehabilitation, or you may end up with a medical problem necessitating a higher level of care. For all these reasons, you would be wise to check out the skilled nursing and rehab facilities in your area.

Last year I had a friend who fell and broke her leg quite badly while chasing her dog in the middle of the night. She had surgery to repair the bone, and then was told to check into a rehab facility for two weeks for extensive physical therapy. Like most healthy sixty-two-year-olds, she knew nothing about rehab hospitals and nursing homes. Because I had recently visited quite a few of the nursing homes (most of which double as rehab hospitals) in our area, I was able to steer her to one that best suited her needs and where I knew she would get good care. Educating yourself about what exists in your neighborhood or town will pay big dividends when the need arises—for you or for a friend.

Like other residential care communities, nursing homes vary in quality and feel. Visit a few. Talk to the people who run them. Look around and get a sense of how the residents are being treated. For a better understanding of skilled nursing and how nursing homes are licensed and run, take a look at the American Health Care Association website (ahca.org), which paints nursing homes in a very positive light and debunks the myths about them as a whole.

One last note about nursing homes today: happily, we are starting to see hints of a quiet revolution in the way nursing homes are set up and managed. In the early 1990s, a physician by the name of Bill Thomas, along with his wife, Jude, founded The Eden Alternative. Dr. Thomas wanted to create a living environment in which residents had more privacy and more control over their lives than they otherwise would in a traditional nursing home. Dr. and Mrs. Thomas started to develop smaller, home-like facilities where residents had private rooms and baths and could move about freely, interacting with other residents and participating in the preparation of meals and the care of plants and resident pets. They called it a "Green House."

The Thomas's first Green House nursing home became wildly successful, by almost any measure you could name. Residents were happier, they were living longer, staff were more engaged with the patients, and employment turnover declined significantly. In 2003, on the heels of their success, Bill and Jude, along with a handful of foundations, started the Green House Project. Today there are hundreds of Green House nursing homes operating or in development in twenty-seven states.43

Once again, if you are currently healthy, this information on the array of residential facilities may seem irrelevant to you. However, consider doing some homework while you are strong and mobile. Visit some nearby assisted living communities, retirement homes, and skilled nursing facilities. They are not all created equal. You are likely to be put off at first if you have never been to one of these establishments, but they serve a very specific need, a need you may eventually have. Have a chat with the executive director or marketing director, and ask questions. Find out the current cost and determine which ones you will most likely be able to afford.

A critical question to ask when you visit these residential communities is, "How heavily do you depend on the families of your residents to pick up the slack in services?" The following are a few more specific questions you should ask:

- How do residents get to doctor appointments?

- How do you obtain residents' medication?

- Who takes the residents to purchase new clothing when necessary?

- Who typically pays the residents' bills and other expenses?

43   "The Green House Project," ChangingAging with Dr. Bill Thomas website, https://changingaging.org/the-green-house-project/.

- Who watches to make sure a resident is not in physical or emotional pain?

- Who ensures that a resident eats properly?

Many of these facilities continue to rely heavily on the families of their residents to pick up the slack in these areas. You may not have family around to fill in, so finding a facility that relies less on outsiders to meet their residents' needs should be an important criterion in the quest.

Want to truly understand how these communities operate on a day-to-day basis? Volunteer at one. There is no better way to understand how they work, what they do, and how they treat their residents. If you are willing to make this additional commitment to understanding these businesses, you will come away with a new and different perspective on them and will be better able to evaluate each one on the considerations important to you.

CHAPTER 22. DOCUMENTING YOUR PREFERENCES FOR CARE

"By failing to prepare, you are preparing to fail."

—Benjamin Franklin

O nce you have made all or most of the decisions described in the chapters on housing, care, and finances, you will want to put them in writing and tell your loved ones about your intentions. These documents and discussions will involve confronting some uncomfortable realities about life ... and death.

I lost my father when I was thirty-eight. I would love to report that he died at home after a week of hospice care, pain-free and surrounded by those he loved. But that's not the way it happened. He was taken to the hospital in an ambulance when, a year after heart-valve transplant surgery, both of his kidneys failed. He was whisked into emergency surgery before I got word of his condition, and neither my brother nor I was able to get to the hospital until the surgery was concluded and he was on a ventilator, a feeding tube, and more IVs than I could count. The nightmare lasted for three weeks.

My father died in 1988. As you will read in Chapter 23, I knew what to do when he died, but I had no idea at the time how to make those final days easier.

There was plenty of technology by then to keep our hearts pumping and our bodies fed and hydrated, but few people knew of any way to let medical professionals know we did not want to end our lives in a hospital critical care unit, hooked up to machines. Thankfully, today we can make those choices beforehand and communicate them to the key people in our lives.

To ensure you are able to conclude your life in a way that resonates with your values and your wishes, let's review the documents you will need to consider in this part of the planning. Depending on the size of your estate, you may not find all of them necessary, but some of them are critical if you want your later-life care wishes carried out. An attorney is the best-qualified person to advise you on these matters.

In the past, people sought out an estate attorney to create a will and a trust and help them decide how to dispose of their money and personal effects after they *died*. Today, we can also document how we want to *live*.

For those without children the important question is, "What happens when I am no longer physically or mentally able to make decisions for myself?" Today, Estate Attorneys, Elder Law Attorneys and Elder Care Attorneys are all designations for legal professionals who will help you determine how to preserve your assets and create the documents that will let a hospital or financial institution know your preferences. They have the specific experience and knowledge required to guide you in developing a state-compliant long-term care plan that will address your financial situation and long-term care goals.

Key documents include:

- Advance health care directive or durable power of attorney for health care (still called a "living will" in some states)

- Durable power of attorney for finances

- Last will and testament

Depending on your financial and marital/familial status, you may also be advised to create a Living Trust. Your attorney will advise you on whether your trust should be "revocable" or "irrevocable." That choice will depend on your age and health at the time you create the document. Once signed, all of these documents become legal and binding. However, reviewing them with your loved ones and an attorney every five years or so is highly recommended. Things can change in your personal life and in the law.

Many decisions have to be made in order to create these documents and the act of creating them will force you to survey your support system and determine who you want to make decisions for you if you are physically and/or mentally unable to make them for yourself.

Advance Health Care Directive

The advance health care directive (AHCD), previously called a "living will," is in most states a binding legal document compelling your "agent" to act according to your wishes. States vary on their interpretation of this document, so it's important to research the conditions in the state where you live. Regardless of your local statute, an AHCD gives you the opportunity to be clear about what you want if you are severely disabled at the end of your life, or for some extended period during your life, and are unable to communicate.

When my father died, being unable to move or speak was not a part of the picture he had foreseen. Had he known he would spend three weeks tied to multiple machines, unable to express even the smallest need to those who cared for him, unable to say goodbye to those who stood helplessly by his bedside, I'm sure he would have chosen a different ending. Today, you can decide what you want to happen in similar circumstances through the use of the AHCD.

Prepare to discuss the AHCD with the person you name as your agent. This person will be much more comfortable knowing your wishes than having to guess what you would want in a stressful moment. When you execute this document you will be making some very specific decisions about the following:

Your personal care:

- Social interaction – With whom and how often?

- Living conditions – Where do you want to receive care?

- Religious or spiritual activity – Do you want visits and/or ministry by clergy or others in your religious circle?

Your health/palliative care:

- Extent of pain relief—what sort of balance do you want between pain relief (which may shorten your life) and the ability to be lucid and communicative?

- Continuation or cessation of hydration and nutrition?

- End-of-life options (life support measures and medication, organ donation)?

Sharing this document with those you have named as agents, as well as your primary care physician or medical group, is critical. Ensure that everyone named in your documents knows they have been named as an agent and has a copy of the document. If possible, go over the document with them, item by item.

Power of Attorney for Finances

A power of attorney (POA) for finances is a simple and reliable way to arrange for another person (called an "agent" or "attorney-in-fact") to manage your finances in the event you become incapacitated and unable to make decisions on your own behalf. Spouses typically name one another during estate planning, so they can act quickly in the event of a sudden incapacitation. Some people even use a POA to allow one spouse to sign documents if the other is out of town. However, in a POA you can name anyone you wish. Your agent does not have to be a spouse or even a relation.

In creating a POA, your attorney will most likely advise you to make it a "durable" power of attorney (DPOA) because in most states, if it is "non-durable," the POA will be *nullified* if you become incapacitated, which will render it useless at the exact time you need it!

A durable power of attorney can be "immediate" or "springing." The term "springing" means it springs into effect at a given point, based on some criteria you define. However, in some states these can be subject to significant delays and can create problems for the agent you name. Your attorney will be able to clarify these points for the state in which you live and steer you in the right direction for your circumstances. If you are married, you may choose a DPOA that goes into effect immediately, so when the time comes, your spouse (as the agent) does not experience any delays in attending to whatever business needs handling. In any case, choose an agent you consider financially savvy and trustworthy to act in your best interest.

When you name someone as your agent, they will have broad power to handle all of your financial transactions. However, you can choose to limit their power to act by specifying the exact transactions for which you want to give your agent authority. The following are typical areas of authority for agents for finances:

- Using your assets to pay expenses you have (or will incur)

- Maintaining your real estate interests by paying the mortgage, taxes, and any other required outlay of funds

- Selling or managing your real estate to cover your expenses

- Transferring property to a trust you previously created

- Collecting Social Security, Medicare, or other government benefits on your behalf

- Managing your retirement accounts and investing your money

- Buying and selling insurance policies and annuities for you

- Operating your business

- Hiring an attorney to represent you in court

- Paying your taxes

- Arranging care for your pets

As your agent, he or she will be required to act in your best interest, maintain accurate records, and keep your property separate from their own.

You can terminate a POA at any time by simply revoking it. When the agent is your spouse, a POA automatically terminates in the case of divorce. A POA ends when you die, so if you want your agent to continue handling your financial affairs *after* you die, you will need to name him/her as the *executor* of your will.

If you are in the early stages of aging and you are healthy, consider naming one or more alternate agents on your AHCD and your POA. For many reasons, your first agent may not be available when needed. There is no limit to how many people you can name as agents in your documents, though you will have to list them in the order you want them to step in for you.

Last Will and Testament

A last will and testament provides instructions for how to dispose of your property after you die. In your will, you can name an executor— the person you want to be responsible for carrying out your wishes. Ultimately, a local court will be responsible for making sure your wishes are carried out as you desire. When you make out a will you must be of "sound mind," so attorneys recommend creating a will at a young age. You can modify a will any time you choose, as often as you choose, as long as your mental faculties are intact.

If you do nothing more than create the documents named above, when you die your estate will be "probated." In some states, probate can be an expensive and time-consuming legal proceeding, in which a designated or appointed attorney will have to prove in a court that your will is valid. Following probate, your property will be inventoried and appraised, your debts and taxes will be paid, and the remaining property distributed according to your will, or according to state law if there is no will. With probate, the cost of the attorney's time, the executor's time and any court fees are paid out of your estate before anything can be distributed to your heirs.

Revocable Trust

To avoid your estate having to be "probated," you will need to create a trust. In states where probate is an expensive and time-consuming process, many people create trusts for the sole purpose of avoiding the probate cost and delay. In addition to avoiding probate and reducing expenses, a trust will ensure your financial affairs remain in the private domain (wills become public record) and will make the administration much simpler. State laws vary on how an individual's affairs are handled after their death. Therefore, I am not going to dive any deeper into the area of trusts, but I encourage you to do some research in your own state to find out how the system works and decide what you will need.

Maggie Brothers, a Santa Rosa, California attorney and a friend, developed the following chart. She suggested I add it to this book, and I happily agreed. You may find it helpful in sorting out the legal terminology of estate and elder care planning. Bear in mind, however, that it is tied to current California law. Your state may use somewhat different wording in their statutes.

		ESTATE PLANNING:
	Trust	**Will**
Title of Agent	Trustee, Co-Trustee, Successor Trustee	Personal representative or administrator. (Commonly called "executor")
Role	Manage the assets in your trust for the benefit of the beneficiaries, both during your life and after your death	Administer your will; represent your interests after your death
When can the agent act?	Both during your life and after your death	Only after death
What does the agent have power over? (examples only)	✔ All assets titled in the name of the Trust	✔ Assets titled in your name which your Will specifies ✔ Death benefits (e.g., from retirement plans) ✔ Assets which do not have a named beneficiary or joint owner ✔ Filing of tax returns and payment of taxes ✔ Payment of your final bills ✔ Representing your interests in a lawsuit filed on your/your estate's behalf or against your estate

Who Does What and When?	
Durable Power of Attorney for Finance & Personal Affairs	Advance Healthcare Directive (CA)
Attorney-in-fact	Agent
Act for you during your life to manage your personal affairs, (such as paying bills) but only when you are incapacitted (unless you grant immediate powers)	Make healthcare decisions for you if you are incapacitated (unless you grant immediate powers)
Only during your life	Mostly during your life
✔ Assets that are in your name (e.g., your day-to-day checking account) ✔ Retirement accounts, IRAs, 401ks, etc. ✔ Your paycheck ✔ Social Security and other government benefits ✔ Filing your tax return ✔ Signing contracts on your behalf ✔ Representing your interests in a lawsuit filed on your behalf or against you as an individual	✔ Consent, refuse consent, or withdraw consent to medical treatment or services ✔ Choose physicians ✔ Consent to the release of medical information ✔ Sign admission papers and related douments ✔ Manage the disposition of your remains after death

While writing this book, my friend Rita had an experience that taught us both some additional lessons about what ends up being important to your agents, your trustees, and your executor when you are gone:

Rita and Lonnie, both child-free women, had known each other for many years and loved and trusted each other implicitly. Although Rita had remarried and moved 150 miles north of Lonnie, they visited each other's homes when they could and stayed in touch. When they were both in their early sixties, they completed the documents recommended by their respective estate attorneys, with Lonnie naming Rita the sole designee (agent) on her AHCD, her DPOA for finances, and as the sole executor of her will. Rita was aware of this.

Soon after retiring in December of 2015, Lonnie reported to Rita that she had updated her documents. Rita suggested they review the documents together, but Lonnie never got around to sending them. In March of 2016, Lonnie developed a respiratory infection that turned into pneumonia. When Rita found out Lonnie had been hospitalized, she rushed to the intensive care unit and made sure the hospital staff knew she was Lonnie's agent. She gave them specific instructions on how to reach her if there was any change in her condition or they had questions about her care. Lonnie deteriorated fast in the ICU, and even though Rita had met with the staff, no one from the hospital ever contacted her to discuss Lonnie's declining condition. Instead, Ronnie got a phone call from the hospital administrator four days later to inform her Lonnie had died.

Lonnie's death kicked off a long and demanding sequence of events that Rita was still trying to manage, six months after her friend's passing, all the while grieving the devastating and sudden loss.

Rita's first job was to give the hospital instructions for disposition of Lonnie's remains. She was listed on Lonnie's durable medical document with a slightly different name (a clerical error by the attorney's office) which led to several difficult hours at the hospital

278

before the hospital would allow Rita to obtain Lonnie's belongings and sign off on disposition of her body. Rita and Lonnie had never discussed what should happen after Lonnie died, and Lonnie had not done any "pre-need" planning, so the decision fell to Rita on how to inter Lonnie's remains. Since she knew Lonnie's parents had been cremated, she chose cremation for Lonnie. Rita had to find and call a mortuary that handled cremation, pay for the services, and begin the laborious process of keeping track of all the expenses involved in the execution of her friend's estate.

Lonnie had a trust, but the trust paperwork had been poorly executed and carried the same erroneous name for Rita as the AHCD. Despite the existence of the trust, Rita could not get access to any of Lonnie's assets to pay bills until she involved a second lawyer to request the court to correct her trust document and house deed to identify Rita correctly as executor. In addition, Lonnie's checking account was not listed as a trust asset, nor was Rita a co-signee on the account, so Rita was not able to pay the outstanding medical and cremation bills with Lonnie's money. She made the decision to pay critical bills for Lonnie's estate out of her own savings, knowing she would not be reimbursed for several months.

In the midst of all the administrative and logistical work, Rita also had to plan a memorial service for her friend, put announcements in the paper, close down her social media accounts, notify everyone in Lonnie's address book, clean out her house, find a home for her cat, and, as executor, manage the sale of her car and her home. The tasks were all-consuming. Had Rita been employed full-time, she would have had to take a leave of absence.

What did Rita and I learn from the experience?

1. Review your documents with your agents when you create them and whenever you update them. If Rita and Lonnie had gone over the papers together, they would have caught the clerical errors that became so troublesome.

2. Someone on your AHCD needs to be local. Rita had trouble communicating with the hospital from a distance. If at all possible, list an agent who is within a thirty-minute drive from the hospital where medical personnel would take you in an emergency.

3. Include your burial or cremation wishes in your documents and do the pre-need planning so you don't leave your agents guessing about what you want and having to foot the bill.

4. If you have set up a trust, put as many of your assets into the trust as you are legally allowed. Trusts are well understood by the legal system in the United States. As the trustee, Rita would have had easier access to the checking account and any other liquid funds in the trust.

5. Provide instructions about what to do for your pets. Arrange for your pet to have a "godparent"—someone who has agreed to take him/her if you predecease them.

6. Divide the work. Because Rita was named as the agent, attorney in fact, and executor, her obligations became a full-time job for several months. If she had selected a relative or another close friend to be her trustee or her agent for finances, leaving Rita to manage the health and disposition decisions, they could have shared the tasks and worked together to accomplish what had to be done.

7. Keep good records. Make lists and familiarize your agent(s) and executor with the whereabouts of all important documents. Include in these records, names and contact information of your CPA (for taxes), your attorney, your primary care physician, and all banking institutions with which you do business. Also include passwords and pin numbers for your social media and financial accounts, ownership deeds, and address book.

8. Keep duplicates of your car keys, the key to your home, and the key to your safe-deposit box (if you have one) with the above documents.

In the wake of this experience, Rita and her husband have put together what they call the "If I croak" list. Those informal pages contain all the information above, and they have given them to each other and to one other person who lives near them. Sound thinking, in my opinion.

Attorneys have told me the safest way to ensure your wishes are honored at a hospital is to arrange for someone to act as your "advocate," someone who can spend as much time as possible in the hospital with you. Of course, that person must also be named as someone who can make decisions on your behalf, so if you and your spouse, friend, or relative agree to be advocates for one another, make sure they are the same person named on your AHCD.

Long-Term Care Plan

All of the above constitutes your long-term care plan from a legal perspective, but I encourage you to go a little further. No matter our age, we all run the risk of being incapacitated to the point where we cannot communicate our needs or wishes. Decisions about how you want to be treated, how pain-free versus alert you'd like to be, and who you want to be near you are some of the questions you will want to consider ahead of time.

There are two excellent organizations that publish resources and worksheets to stimulate your thinking and allow you to put these preferences on paper (or online). The "Five Wishes" document has been around for over a decade and is recognized in most states as a binding legal document that can serve as your AHCD. Five Wishes is published by Aging with Dignity. Five Wishes documents can be accessed online or ordered in paper version at agingwithdignity.org.

Another excellent resource for end-of-life planning resources and information is Compassion and Choices *(compassionandchoices.org)*. They produce a useful booklet, the *Good-To-Go Resource Guide*. They cover the basics of an advance directive and the decisions you should make. The booklet also describes the kinds of life support treatment you might receive in a hospital, unless you legally request treatment be withheld. These include artificial ventilation and the intravenous administration of food and water. Compassion and Choices also provides excellent guidance on how to start the conversation with loved ones and those you are naming in your documents as agents.

Compassion and Choices has an excellent page on their website which contains specific guidance for the LGBTQ community. Although as of this writing lesbian and gay seniors are able to take advantage of much more enlightened practices—by both the medical and legal communities—they still face many more hurdles than their straight counterparts, especially with regard to end-of-life issues. Good planning and legally tight documents are critical.

Feeling squeamish about all this? Here is what happens if you become incapacitated and you have not executed these documents: a court judge will put your case into a conservatorship and will appoint someone (a conservator or guardian) to make decisions on your behalf—a "paid guardian." The court may not appoint the person *you* would have selected, especially if they are not related to you or named in any document. The decisions the conservator makes for your care may be totally different from what you would have chosen for yourself. No matter how vehemently your loved ones argue on your behalf, the conservator will make decisions independently, or in conjunction with a court judge—based on *their own* belief system and preferences.

The following worksheet, Ensuring a Secure Future, will give you an opportunity to look at what you have done to secure your future in this way, and what you still need to do.

Ensuring a Secure Future

Legal Documents	What It Does	Your Plan
Will	Provides instruction to the courts for disposal of your property through probate.	
Trust (Revocable Living Trust is the popular instrument today)	Avoids probate and makes disposition of your property much quicker and less expensive.	
Advance health care directive (AHCD), also called a living will	Legal document in which you specify what actions should be taken for your health if you are unable to make decisions for yourself because of illness or incapacity. Even a SPOUSE cannot make decisions for you without it!	
Durable power of attorney (DPOA) for health decisions	Generally goes hand-in-hand with the AHCD; allows you to authorize someone (an agent) to sign your name and make decisions on your behalf when you are incapacitated.	

Legal Documents	What It Does	Your Plan
Durable power of attorney (DPOA) for finance decisions	Allows you to authorize someone (an agent) to sign your name and make decisions of a legal or financial nature (for non-trust assets) on your behalf when you are incapacitated.	
Long-term care plan	Stipulates the location and delivery preferences for long-term care if/when that becomes necessary.	

Other Planning	What It Does	Your Plan
Financial savings and retirement plan	Gives you peace of mind that you will be on solid financial footing for the rest of your life	
Getting your records in order	Avoids confusion and mistaken assumptions	
Family discussions to communicate your wishes	Avoids surprise, heartache, and unexpected decision-making at a maximally stressful time	
Long-term care insurance	Protects your assets from being depleted by long-term care costs	

If you are married or have a life partner, you will likely select your spouse/partner as the primary "agent" or appointee for your health care decisions. Your attorney will strongly encourage you to name at least one other person, and even a third, in case your spouse and the first designee predecease you or become incapacitated. Singles should also name secondary and tertiary agents in their planning.

If you come from a large family and are close to your siblings and their children, you have the advantage of a long-term, well-known support system. Your job will be to choose the ones you are closest to or the ones you see as the most stable, adding them as agents in your documents and having a discussion with them about what you have done, why you have done it, and what you expect of them. On the other hand, what if you do not have a close-knit family? What if they live in another country? What if your family members have values so different from yours that you would rather not name any of them as your agent? Now you must select among your friends, and that sets up a dilemma if all your friends are around your same age.

Finding a Younger Support System

"It will never rain roses: when we want to have more roses, we must plant more trees."

—George Eliot

If you are among the many child-free baby boomers who have spent their entire lives associating with like-minded, like-aged people, *now* is the time to step out of that box. Begin by looking around you. Where are the younger people who might share some of your interests and become trusted friends? Here are some places to look for them:

- Your nieces and nephews

- Children of your close friends

- Younger coworkers

- Younger church/synagogue/mosque members

- Younger people on civic committees or boards on which you serve

- Neighbors who are younger

- Younger participants in organizations or clubs to which you belong (e.g., book clubs, hiking clubs, quilting clubs, professional associations, travel groups, homeowner associations, meetups that are not age-centric, etc.)

Okay, maybe you know some younger people, but how do you go from knowing who they are to becoming close enough to ask them to be an agent on one or more of your estate and long-term care planning documents? Time and cultivation. Relationships are like plants. In the same way a tomato seed becomes a bountiful plant providing luscious fruit throughout the summer, a single handshake can, over time, become a rewarding friendship for both of you. A friendship takes longer to grow than a tomato, so you will need to invest *years* in this process. Hopefully, those years will be rewarding and enjoyable for both of you. Another reason to start NOW.

Begin by finding reasons to spend time together. Since you know them through a common group or third person, start there. Here are some ideas:

- Make an effort to attend gatherings you know they attend.

- Invite them to a gathering you are having at your home or are sponsoring elsewhere.

- Suggest meeting for coffee to discuss something you have in common or a problem you believe they can help you with.

- Learn more about their life by asking open questions when you are together for a common event.

People like to talk about their interests, thoughts, opinions, experience, etc. If you choose a shy person, you may need to expend more effort to draw them out. Reluctance to engage in conversation doesn't mean they don't like you; they may be awkward in social situations or not adept at interpersonal dialogue.

Depending on the personality of the person or persons you have selected, you may have to work harder in the initial stages of your relationship. Even if you have known the young person for a long time, you may still need to develop an adult-to-adult relationship and bring them into your circle of trusted friends. This young person should have the potential of becoming a lifelong friend. Even though most of your wishes will be spelled out in the documents already mentioned, only with familiarity and a true friendship will they feel confident having your power of attorney and believing they understand your values and what you want in your oldest years.

Hiring a Professional

If you have gotten to this point in the chapter and are still uneasy about whom you could name as your agent, you may want to consider a *professional* to take over your affairs and your decision-making if you become incapable of doing so yourself. You may have heard the word "guardian" or "conservator." These are the terms used by the courts when they are petitioned to appoint a caretaker for an individual who has demonstrated that they can no longer safely care for themselves or make sound decisions. This usually follows a crisis of some sort, like the discovery of an older person falling prey to a financial scam or having suffered an acute medical event (heart attack, stroke, etc.).

Today, an increasing number of forward-thinking people are being proactive in seeking out a professional private guardian—someone they have met and with whom they are comfortable—to take over their affairs if they become unable to care for themselves and manage their lives in a safe and secure manner. In most states this professional is referred to as a private guardian. The word "private" denotes an individual, as opposed to a court of law, has engaged them. In a few states (e.g., California and Arizona) you would seek out a "professional fiduciary." However, guardian is still the term a court or attorney in any jurisdiction will understand.

What do they do? A professional guardian is an individual who assumes a position of responsibility and trust over the affairs of a person who can no longer act in their own behalf. As the number of people living with significant cognitive impairment grows, so has the need for these professionals, and their ranks have swelled. Often appointed by probate court, the professional guardian is charged with the responsibility of carrying out the terms of a Living Trust and managing many of the day-to-day affairs of individuals who can no longer do so for themselves. Being a competent professional guardian is a complex job and may require expertise in the law, accounting, real estate, taxes, and more. The duties of a professional guardian may include:

- Supervising medical care, insurance benefits, and disability benefits

- Arranging a living facility

- Managing personal care needs

- Arranging meals and appropriate clothing

- Managing home care services

- Arranging housekeeping or groundkeeping services

- Arranging and managing transportation services and daily activities

- Supporting spiritual beliefs and acting in accordance with them

- Managing financial assets

- Providing recordkeeping and accounting

- Assuring federal and local tax returns are filed

- Coordinating a team of professional services as needed

You may never need all of these services, but in the event you do, you will want to consider whom you trust to make these kinds of arrangements for you on an ongoing basis, potentially for months or years. It can be a full-time job for several months. If you have a family member or friend you think would perform these duties for you, it's best to have a conversation with them in advance to make sure they are willing and able.

Rob and Karen live in Phoenix, Arizona. They are Solo Agers in their mid-sixties and have spent the last six years managing the care and, finally, the estate of Rob's father. They found the many tasks time-consuming and challenging. Rob had his father's DPOA for both health care and finances, so they were able to effect his transition to a nursing home in his last eight months, and one or both of them stayed in close contact with the facility to ensure he was well cared for. However, once he died and the initial tasks of interment and funeral service were behind them, they spent another year resolving his will and trust. Those tasks were tedious and included paying the final medical bills, organizing the sale of the house, disposing of his possessions, executing his wishes for donations and charitable contributions, closing his accounts, selling his car, and handling all correspondence with family and friends.

Rob and Karen experienced firsthand what it takes to settle an estate. They decided they could not ask any of their friends to take on such a monumental task when they are gone, or even beforehand when the main task would involve managing care—for one or both of them. When they explained this to their accountant, she recommended a professional fiduciary and gave them the name of one she had worked with and trusted.

The next week they made an appointment to meet the fiduciary. After their first meeting, they agreed they liked him and began what they hoped would be a long-term relationship. They met with their estate attorney and named the fiduciary as an agent in several places in their estate documents. The fiduciary is now named as the executor on each of their wills and successor trustee (after one another) on their trust. He is also named as tertiary on both of their advance directives for health care and will fill in if needed.

Fiduciaries charge by the hour. Rob and Karen have decided to pay her hourly fee to meet with them once a year in order to communicate any changes in their health or their estate plans and continue the process of trust-building. Their attorney recommended they name a second fiduciary as a backup and they have done that as well.

If the idea of giving your power of attorney to a professional appeals to you, take time to do some research and be selective about whom you engage for this role. Consider interviewing several individuals. Select the one with whom you feel the most comfortable (and whose references are impeccable). You can then name them to act as your agent to manage your estate and your personal affairs, and make medical and care decisions should you become mentally or physically incapacitated. They will become the "agent" in your durable power of attorney (DPOA) and/or your AHCD documents. You can appoint them as co-agents with a friend or relative you trust, and you can also give them partial powers to do specific things for you, all of which must be specified in your documents.

Some of the questions you will want to ask your potential guardian or fiduciary are the following:

- What services do you offer? What are your hours?

- How long have you been practicing and what issues have you encountered and solved?

- Are you bonded? Insured? Certified by the National Guardian Association (NGA) or licensed as a professional fiduciary?

- If you have a staff, what do you delegate to them? What kind of background checks have been done on your staff, and what insurance do you have for employee theft and liability?

- Do you have knowledge of the medical issues I am facing or may face?

- What knowledge and connections do you have of local service providers I may need (e.g., caregivers, housekeepers, nurses)?

- What security measures do you have in place to protect my information?

- If a natural disaster occurs, what plans are in place for resuming business as quickly as possible? Do you have a disaster recovery plan for my data?

- What is your succession plan in the event you die or become incapacitated before me?

- How do I reach you or your staff after hours?

- What contingency plans do you have in place for your vacations or unexpected illnesses?

- What are your fees and when are they billed?

In addition to asking the above questions, I strongly encourage you to ask for references. Once you have the contacts, email or call them to set up a time to talk about their experience with your prospective guardian.

Of course, you don't want your agent to act on your behalf on any matters you are still capable of handling, so be certain to specify in your documents how the decision to turn over these responsibilities will be handled. For instance, at age eighty-five, you may be more than ready to turn over your insurance management, bill paying, and the hiring and coordination of your care team. You may not want to relinquish decisions about how you manage your financial assets, where you live, and what clothing you need. You should be the one to decide what you are ready to turn over. The one exception to the above is signs of dementia. You must understand that anyone who interacts with you on a regular basis may recognize this, contact others who care about you, and together, with your best interests in mind, ask your primary care physician to provide the signature to have you placed under the full care of the guardian or fiduciary you have named in your legal documents. Realize, though, if you show signs of being unable to manage your life and you have not selected a fiduciary or guardian in advance, a court will put you in the hands of a stranger. I'd rather know in advance who my guardian will be, wouldn't you?

Guardians and fiduciaries charge by the hour. They get paid when their services are needed. Since most of their time is back-end loaded, the majority of their fee will come out of your estate at the time they become active as your agent. However, I encourage you to consider paying for a yearly meeting, as Rob and Karen are doing, so they can get to know you as well as possible. The better they know you, the more confident they will feel that your needs are being met by their decisions, and the more confident you will feel that they will make the right decisions for you. Even for those who have family in the picture, an independent, impartial professional can often act more logically and more quickly than someone close to you.

Finding a professional guardian or fiduciary who works in the private sector in your area should not be difficult if you approach the search in the same way you would if you were looking for a competent doctor or dentist. Start by asking people you know. Other good sources are the National Guardianship Association (guardianship.org) and the Professional Fiduciary Associations in states where fiduciaries are licensed. If you have a personal attorney, they will be able to connect you with at least one such professional. Because guardians are often appointed to manage the personal and monetary affairs of their clients, most attorneys build relationships with one or more in their areas of practice. Your attorney (or someone in their office) may also be willing to perform those tasks, but a guardian makes their living that way and often charges far less than an attorney or even a legal assistant. Professional guardians often use a website as their marketing tool, so you might start your search online.

> Search by the name of your town plus the term "professional guardian," "private guardian," or "professional fiduciary."

In some states (e.g., California) the profession of fiduciary is a *licensed* occupation. If your state doesn't have a licensure program for fiduciaries or guardians, be sure they are insured and bonded. In addition, the Center for Guardianship Certification (CGC) administers a national certification program for guardians, fiduciaries, and conservators. A guardian who can furnish evidence of being certified (an NCG) will have passed eligibility standards which include a minimum level of knowledge and experience in guardianship services. However, even with this certification, check the guardian's references in the community and their standing in the local Better Business Bureau.

A "Daily Money Manager" (DMM) is another professional who may interest you if you like the idea of a more limited scope for the person you engage. Sometimes they work in tandem with a guardian or fiduciary, but they can also be hired on their own. A DMM provides personal business assistance to clients who have difficulty managing their personal monetary affairs. Their services include organizing and tracking medical insurance papers, maintaining bank accounts (deposits and withdrawals), and assisting with check writing to pay bills and other expenditures. DMMs have a more diverse client base, often working with busy executives and over-extended professionals. Their senior client base consists mainly of people who have limited vision, limited mobility, or other physical or mental conditions that make it difficult for them to keep up with their financial affairs. However, younger seniors sometimes hire them to attend to financial matters while they are on extended globe-trotting expeditions. A DMM handles any of the following tasks, as requested or required:

- Bill paying and preparation of checks for clients to sign

- Balancing checkbooks and maintaining organization of bank records

- Preparing and delivering bank deposits

- Organizing tax documents and related paperwork

- Negotiating with creditors

- Deciphering medical insurance papers and tracking the processing of claims

- Some DMMs will also provide related services, such as:

- Referrals to legal, tax, and investment professionals

- Notarizing documents

- Maintaining home payroll records (e.g., for the care team), including calculation of federal and state withholding and FICA taxes

- Transportation to and from appointments, shopping, etc.

- Assistance with relocation

- Acting as the agent or representative payee for Medicare

As you can see from the description, a DMM has fewer powers to act on your behalf than someone with a complete power of attorney or an individual you have selected to be your guardian. However, at some point in the future a DMM may be all you need in your circumstances.

As with all of the professionals described in this book, you should check their references and background, assure they are licensed, bonded, certified by the appropriate accrediting body, and have been in the business for at least ten years.

Creating a Planning Kit

Even if you are diligent in attending to all the suggestions in this chapter, they won't be of much value if no one can find the information or documents when they are needed. To that end, it will be to everyone's advantage to have it all collected in one place in your home or on your computer. Consider putting together a *Personal Life Planning Portfolio*. Here is what it should contain:

Contact information: Include close family members and/or anyone named on your advance directive, one or two friends, your attorney, your fiduciary (if applicable), your financial advisor, tax preparer, and anyone you have selected (and talked to) about pet or home care.

Health information: Include all conditions you are managing, a list of all medications, and contact info for doctors and pharmacies. Create a list of important documents and where they are located. This should include your advance directive, will, trust, and all insurance policies.

Financial information: Include a list of banks and any other institutions where you have accounts, brokerage firms, and credit card companies. Include all account numbers.

Property information: Include a list of your property holdings and copies of titles.

End-of-life information: Include a copy of any funeral information, burial plot purchase contracts or cremation service agreements, and any last wishes you wish to convey.

Avoiding "Elder Abuse"

There is no foolproof way of knowing if someone is going to treat you badly, mismanage your affairs, steal from you, or even hurt you, but as a society we have safeguards and we should utilize them as best we can. Abuse can take many forms, including self-neglect, which encompasses an older individual's unwillingness or inability to care for themselves. The majority of abuse claims reported to Adult Protective Services occur in domestic settings, as opposed to a facility for older adults.[44] That statistic goes along with the surprising finding that family members are the most frequent perpetrators of abuse, especially where an older family member resides in the home of the relative who is the sole or primary caregiver.

Physical or sexual abuse is the most commonly recognized form of elder abuse. However, other kinds of abuse are more likely in the case of someone without children, since few of us end up living with relatives who can wield that kind of power.

- **Psychological or emotional abuse** is inflicted through intimidation or stories provoking emotional anguish. Family members or those who have been close to the victim in the past most often inflict this kind of abuse.

- **Neglect** is most often manifested in the failure of a caregiver—paid or volunteer—to provide the necessities of life to their charge. Withholding food, water, medicine, clothing, or personal hygiene are all forms of neglect, as are the failure to provide adequate safety or shelter, or the shirking of financial responsibilities. The perpetrator in these cases may be a relative or someone who has been paid to deliver the service but has failed to do so adequately.

---

44   "Elder Abuse Facts," National Council on Aging website, https://www.ncoa. org/public-policy-action/elder-justice/elder-abuse-facts/.

- **Financial or material exploitation** is the illegal or inappropriate use of an older person's resources. This kind of abuse may involve appropriation of funds through illegal writing of checks, illegal sale or management of property, or misrepresentation of the older person's intentions through coercing their signature or impersonation of the older person in some manner.

Unfortunately, older adults are frequent targets for scams that take the form of phony telemarketing, bogus Internet offers, and investment fraud. In today's world, guarding against these kinds of schemes is difficult for a person of *any* age. Checking out the legitimacy of offers we receive by mail or email has become increasingly challenging. As we age, we will be the targets of these scam artists with greater frequency; MetLife research reports that older adults were the target of 80 percent of the solicitation calls. If you live alone, you will be an even greater temptation for these unscrupulous thieves and racketeers. The following are some safeguards you can employ. They will make you less vulnerable to scam solicitations:

- Use caller ID to screen calls, and do not pick up the phone if you do not recognize the caller's name or number.

- Let your answering device pick up any call you are not expecting. A legitimate caller will leave a message.

- If you do pick up the phone and the caller is someone you don't know, hang up immediately.

- Delete all solicitation emails.

- Add your name to the National Do Not Call Registry by calling 1-888-382-1222 or by going online to donotcall.gov.

- Install malware and other safeguards on your computer (e.g., *LifeLock*) to prevent ID theft.

Beyond these mechanical safeguards, you can protect yourself by staying social and avoiding isolation. Stay in touch with family members and friends, make new friends wherever possible, volunteer where and when you can, and participate in group activities with your religious or spiritual community. Be cautious when making a financial decision. Discuss your plans with others you trust and get feedback before acting. Be sure to safeguard your financial documents by keeping them in a secure location and by making sure loved ones have copies. Never give out your passwords to anyone. Beware of any person (even a family member) who suggests you add their name to your bank accounts or property title or asks you to co-sign a loan. Also, beware of anyone who suggests you change your will in any way. AARP has a Fraud Watch Network link on their website.[45] You can use it to track the latest scams and alert you to the most common ones in your area. AARP's Fraud Watch Network includes a phone number you can call to talk to a trained volunteer who will help you evaluate whether you are facing a scam situation.[46]

These are precautionary measures everyone should take. There are plenty of scam artists out there, but there are also lots of good, caring people in the world who want to ensure your happiness, well-being, and security. This section was not written to scare you into worrying every time you answer the phone or want to investigate a new opportunity to make a friend. It is a reminder of the need for vigilance in our personal lives as we get older.

PLEASE NOTE: I am not an attorney. In this chapter I have provided ideas and opinions about how to prepare for a time when you may not be able to manage your personal affairs. I strongly encourage you to seek out professional advice from an elder law attorney, estate attorney, or legal aid society in your state before acting on any of the ideas or suggestions mentioned in the stories or narrative of this chapter.

---

45   As of writing, the AARP's Fraud Watch website is at *http://aarp.org/money/scams-fraud/fraud-watch-network/*.

46   As of writing, the AARP Fraud Watch Helpline is 1-877-908-3360.

CHAPTER 23. END-OF-LIFE CHOICES

"To laugh often and much; to win the respect of intelligent people and the affection of children ... to leave the world a better place ... to know even one life has breathed easier because you have lived. This is to have succeeded."

—Ralph Waldo Emerson

Sometime during my college days, when I was home for a visit with my recently-divorced father, then in his late fifties, he asked me to sit down for a talk about his end-of-life plan. He had been to his attorney to update his will and wanted to discuss it with me. I told him I had no interest in talking about death, especially his, but no matter how hard I tried to get out of the discussion, he prevailed and we had the first of several conversations reviewing his pre-need planning and the list of things I should do upon learning of his death.

My father had named me as executor in his will and was very specific about what he expected of me. As circumstances shifted (grandchildren were born, ex-wives died), we had more of these discussions over the next eighteen years. With repetition and desensitization, I eventually heard and absorbed what he was saying. When he passed away at age seventy-five, I knew how to locate all the important documents and was familiar with the cemetery where his pre-purchased plot and casket were ready for him. I was able to schedule a memorial service as he wanted, and invite the people he wanted to be there. Even during the worst of the shock and grief over his death, his planning was so thorough I was able to carry out his wishes without a hitch. His planning was the kindest, most loving thing he could have done.

I learned two important lessons from the experience with my father. The first: we need to create a plan for that final stage of life. The second: no matter how vehemently loved ones resist, discussing end-of-life plans with those who will be responsible for carrying them out is a loving gesture. Those of us who do not have adult children need to select the right people for this responsibility and dive fearlessly into these discussions.

Elisabeth Kübler-Ross, in her pioneering work on the end of life,[47] informed us about the stages people pass through as they approach the final transition of life and the concerns they expressed when asked about their experience. In the middle of the twentieth century, when Kübler-Ross conducted her study, people didn't talk about death—ever. That taboo seems to be ebbing. There is a movement afoot to bring end-of-life conversations out in the open. Since death is the last taboo topic in our modern culture, the more we become comfortable talking about how we feel about our own death and how we want to spend our final days, the better prepared we will be when that time comes— no matter how old we are.

The controversial "death with dignity" movement, to allow individual choice about when and where we die, is gaining steam in many states. The growing trend among people who subscribe to a more secular way of life is for humans to be legally allowed to end their life on their own terms. The "death with dignity" movement (the term "assisted suicide" is now shunned) is heavily backed by baby boomers who watched their parents or grandparents suffer and finally succumb to slow, painful illnesses. There are others, however, who are deeply opposed to this path. They maintain the belief that God has a plan for them and it is not their place to alter that plan.

---

47   Elizabeth Kübler-Ross, On Death and Dying: What the Dying Have to Teach Doctors, Nurses, Clergy, & their Own Families (New York: Scribner, 1969).

No matter which path you choose for yourself, communicating your wishes to those close to you, especially those who will likely outlive you, is critical. Both the Compassion and Choices information and The Five Wishes document can help you think through this issue and prepare for the conversations.

Several grassroots organizations are promoting group discussions about death. Death Cafe (deathcafe.com) is the best known at this time. It started in London, and Death Cafe discussions are now growing in popularity in Western Europe, Australasia, and the United States. The people who manage the Death Cafe website and Facebook page call Death Cafe a "social franchise." They give permission to use the term "Death Cafe" to anyone who follows the guidelines on their website. There they explain how to host and facilitate a meeting, and how to publicize and promote it. To date there have been over five thousand Death Cafes in fifty-two countries around the world. The only continent that has so far not experienced on is Antarctica. People can attend just once or make the meetings a steady diet. The rules for facilitation are simple and basic:

- The meetings must be free to attend (a small contribution for food is allowed).

- No one may be prevented from attending.

- There must be no "experts" or "speakers."

- There must be food of some sort (cookies, cake, crackers and cheese, etc.).

- No one is allowed to "sell" any particular idea or belief.

The founders also encourage posting any Death Cafe meetings on their website and contributing a few sentences about the experience.

Discussions about death are increasingly appearing in the media. In 2013, PBS aired *Homegoings*, an hour-long documentary on the life of an African-American funeral director, as part of the network's acclaimed

POV (Point of View) nonfiction film series. The website for *Homegoings* (pbs.org/pov/homegoings/) has a variety of information and resources on the topic of death and funeral arrangements, including a section entitled "Discussions About Death."

Alternatively, you may not feel you need any guidance to have a discussion with your friends about death. You may want to leave the format casual and let the conversation go where it will. If you choose an unstructured approach, the following questions may be helpful as conversation starters:

- Why do you think so many people are uncomfortable talking about death?

- What, if any, are your family traditions when people die?

- What are your fears about death?

- What is your ideal way to die?

- Do you want a traditional funeral service or something unique?

- What do you want done with your body when you die? Do you prefer cremation or burial?

- What are some of the grieving experiences you have had or seen in others?

- What role can social media presence play in the grieving process?

The more we know about our own wishes and those of others in our social network, the better prepared we will be for this final experience. Once you are more confident of what you want, be sure to record your wishes as an addendum to your will *and* your advance directive.

One final decision to make is how you want your remains treated after your death. In the story about my father, I mentioned he had done all the groundwork ahead of time for his own death. He had purchased a plot in a cemetery, picked out his coffin, paid the burial fee ahead of time, and had the important discussion with me about where to find the paperwork. He also took me to the cemetery and showed me the burial plot. This interaction wasn't easy for him or for me, but it was immeasurably helpful to me when the time came.

There are other options available for final disposition of your remains. Cremation has been around for thousands of years longer than burial, and there has been a resurgence in its popularity for several reasons. Some religious denominations that had previously banned cremation have recently declared it acceptable. Additionally, burial land is getting scarcer, especially in urban areas, and people are becoming more aware of the need for conservation. The Neptune Society, a nationwide organization with a stellar reputation throughout their forty years, provides advanced planning options for people who wish to prepay for cremation services. Their package includes transport of the remains, the cremation service, a container for the ashes, and disposition of the ashes at sea. Similar companies exist throughout the United States and Western Europe.

"Green burial" is another option today. Green or natural burial involves minimal impact on the environment and aids in the conservation of the surrounding natural resources. Caskets, shrouds or urns must be made of biodegradable and nontoxic materials. Green burial proponents discourage the use of embalming fluid as unnecessary and carcinogenic in nature. There are a limited number of places certified for green burial, so if this concept interests you, start your planning early and learn all you can about the process and its limitations.

You may also want to plan your own funeral in advance, if you would rather not leave it to chance or burden your loved ones at a stressful time. You can choose the venue for your service, write your own eulogy, and choose the music. You may also want to ask specific people to speak at your funeral. This kind of planning is common among people who have a slow-growing terminal illness and have the time to think and plan.

Remember my friend Sondra from the story in Chapter 7? She was the one who left me the rich legacy of how to be my best self with my clients. By the time she left us, she had known she was dying for almost three years. In the final months of her battle with ovarian cancer, she had completely accepted her own death and was ready for it. Hospice was there with her family and me to help ease her transition.

During the final month, at times when her pain was well controlled and she was lucid enough to think clearly, she made her own funeral plans. She talked and I was the scribe. She chose the church, the pallbearers, the songs, and wrote the death notice for the local paper. She asked me to email or call those she wanted to speak at her service, and she wrote a final message to be read during the service as part of her eulogy. She approached this whole process in quite a matter-of-fact manner. The discussion didn't feel maudlin, and Sondra wasn't morose. She wasn't afraid to die; death, for her, was one more passage in what had been a full and rewarding life.

As Kübler-Ross found in her research, when a dying person has reached the stage of "acceptance," they are comfortable with this kind of planning and the discussions accompanying it. Those who are at the bedside as these plans are communicated will experience the emotional difficulty more acutely. I certainly found that to be the case.

CHAPTER 24. CONCLUSION

"Live as if you were to die tomorrow. Learn as if you were to live forever."

—Mahatma Gandhi

Now it's up to you. You have the opportunity to plan for a safe and secure older age—a future that won't unduly burden your family, your friends, or your community. You can start now to build a social support system that will keep you engaged, involved, and enjoying life to the greatest extent possible. Talk with your friends and family and plan together. Let them know you are thinking about your future and not leaving things to chance. If you have a partner or spouse, talk to them and negotiate areas where you think differently about your future. You don't have to agree on everything, you just have to communicate so you are aware of each other's dreams and wishes.

There has never been a time in history with more options for older adults. Think of your life as unfolding in stages. If you are relatively healthy today in your fifties, sixties, or seventies, use this time to do your planning and enjoy an active life. Get fit (or fitter) and get that yearly physical. Find something meaningful to do that uses your brain, keeps you engaged, and produces an income if necessary. Be flexible in how you look at the possibilities. Work, volunteer, travel, teach, write ... or cobble together a combination of pastimes that works for you. Enjoy these bonus years, a stage of life that most of our ancestors never had.

Find a safe and secure place to age that is affordable for you. Get out and do some research in your area. You don't have to move there tomorrow, but consider it part of your plan. If you are determined to stay in your home, make the necessary modifications and be knowledgeable about what's around you.

305

Prepare—verbally, legally, financially, and mentally—for a time when you may need help to manage your life. Help is available in many forms. Your local Area Agency on Aging is a terrific resource for housing, legal services, support systems, activities, and referrals. They will know if there is a village or neighborhood senior center that serves older adults in your area, and what state or county programs are available to you. The AARP website is a treasure trove of resources nationwide. Take a look at the many opportunities available to you for forming community—both online and in person. Check out the travel options and the local discounts. Find more affordable insurance options, and keep track of the changes in Medicare and Medicaid.

The chart on the following page captures all the planning categories reviewed in the book. Let it be your guide for taking action in as many areas as you can. No need to start at the top; you can dive in anywhere you like. Alternatively, you may want to modify this checklist or create your own. For some people a journal is a more appealing vehicle for recording your research and tracking your progress in planning. Do it your way, but do it! Exploring your options and having the conversations will raise your comfort level with the whole idea of aging and the changes that accompany this natural process. And one thing I can promise you: you will have lots of company along the way.

A Final Checklist and Guide for Your Planning:

		Further action or notes:	
Finance	Meet with financial advisor	☐	
	Explore long-term care insurance	☐	
	Social Security decision	☐	
	Income sources (list):		
Legal	Advance health care directive (AHCD) or POA for health care decisions	☐	
	POA for finance	☐	
	Will	☐	
	Trust	☐	
Current Housing Preference	Retirement community (local)	☐	
	Retirement community (non-local)	☐	
	Live with others	☐	
	Cohousing or other collaborative arrangement	☐	
	Live alone	☐	

		Further action or notes:
Future Housing Research	Continuing care retirement communities (CCRC)	Date and place visited:
	Assisted living facilities	Date and place visited:
	Board and care homes	Date and place visited:
	Nursing homes	Date and place visited:
	Villages or neighborhood services	What's available:
Health	I get a yearly physical	☐
	I get a yearly dental checkup	☐
	I have a fitness regimen	☐
	I get at least eight hours of sleep a night	☐
	I follow a low-sugar, high-fiber diet	☐
	My water intake is at least two quarts per day	☐
	I get a flu shot	☐
	I get other immunizations (shingles, pneumonia)	☐

		Further action or notes:
Community and Social Support	Sources of community and social support (list):	
Conversations	Spouse	☐
	Other family	☐
	Friends	☐

RESOURCES

AARP (AARP.org)

If you don't yet belong to AARP, join today! At $15 a year, it's one of the best bargains around and you will enjoy benefits that will go way beyond the money. It is the best single source for information on all aspects of retirement and aging that I am aware of. You may not always agree with their political stands, but they have a huge presence in Washington, DC, where they lobby Congress for programs that promote and enhance the lives of seniors. They are, without a doubt, the gorilla in the marketplace for older adults.

AARPs aggressive fundraising, paid advertising, and the dues they collect allow them to do their work, which includes a massive website. It is one of the richest, deepest, most informative sites I have ever encountered. Here is a sample of what you will find:

- Discounts on restaurants, clothing, drugs, services, travel, entertainment, and much more
- Publications (print and online) with articles, interviews, and news, plus online how-to videos
- Buying guides for appliances, cars, and insurance
- Volunteer opportunities
- Fraud alerts
- Health and wellness information
- Care resources
- Travel information
- Career information with job-search tools
- Financial and insurance products and budgeting tools
- Housing information

- Brain Health Assessment and "Staying Sharp" resources
- Local community and state programs

In addition, AARP has co-branded many fine books, some of which are listed in the reference pages in the next section.

Financial Planning Association (FPA) Planner Search
(PlannerSearch.org)

The FPA is the number one place for finding a financial planner in your community. When you enter your city, you will see a list of the Certified Financial Planners (CFP) within a specified distance from where you live. Each listing has a bio and picture. Interview several to find one that feels like a good fit for you.

Elder Law and Estate Planning

(FindLaw.com) You can learn more about legal specialties and find an elder law or estate planning attorney at this site.
(LawHelp.org) This site provides general information about low-cost legal services.

Area Agencies on Aging

Thanks to the Older Americans Act, every state must provide service centers for older adults in their communities. In many states, these service centers are called Councils on Aging. Your state may call them by a slightly different name, but they will have low-cost or free legal help available to adults over fifty-five.

National Association of Area Agencies on Aging (n4a.org)

Area Agencies on Aging (AAAs) make up a network of 600+ organizations nationwide. They serve older adults (60+) in their specific local areas, generally neighboring counties or parishes, but some offer services statewide, especially in sparsely populated areas.

All AAAs offer the following basic services:

311

- **Nutrition** – counseling; home-delivered and congregate (group) meals

- **Caregiver Support** – respite care and caregiver training

- **Information and Referral** – information about assistance programs and referrals to administrators

- **Long-term Care Support & Information** – information about local facilities and investigation of complaints

- **Insurance Counseling** – help for older adults in understanding and utilizing their benefits, with a focus on Medicare

- **Transportation Coordination** – information about public transit and senior transportation options

In most areas, AAAs are the best place to start when looking for support for the above services. In addition, AAA staff members are also widely knowledgeable about other community and public services that the AAA doesn't provide.

REFERENCES &
RECOMMENDED READING

Aging Without Children: European and Asian Perspectives. Edited by Philip Kreager and Elisabeth Schroder-Butterfill. Oxford: Bergahn Books, 2004.

Aging with Dignity. *Five Wishes Document: Helps you Control How You are Treated if You Get Seriously Ill.* http://AgingWithDignity.org/.

Astor, Bart. *AARP Roadmap for the Rest of Your Life: Smart Choices About Money, Health, Work, Lifestyle … and Pursuing Your Dreams.* Hoboken, NJ: John Wiley & Sons, 2013.

Alboher, Marci. *The Encore Career Handbook: How to Make a Living and a Difference in the Second Half of Life.* New York: Workman Publishing, 2013.

Audacious Aging. Edited by Stephanie Marohn. Self-published by the editor, 2008.

Baker, Beth. *With a Little Help from Our Friends: Creating Community as We Grow Older.* Nashville, TN: Vanderbilt Univ. Press: 2014.

Bolles, Richard. *What Color is Your Parachute? A Practical Manual for Job-Hunters and Career-Changers.* New York: Ten Speed Press, 2013.

Bratter, Bernice, and Helen Dennis. *Project Renewment: The First Retirement Model for Career Women.* New York: Scribner, 2008.

Bridges, William. *Managing Transitions: Making the Most of Change,* 2nd ed. Boston, MA: Da Capo Press, 2003.

Carstensen, Laura L. *A Long Bright Future.* New York: Broadway Books, 2009.

Collamer, Nancy. *Second Act Careers: 50+ Ways to Profit from Your Passions During Semi-Retirement*. New York: Ten Speed Press. 2013.

Connidis, Ingrid Arnet. *Family Ties and Aging*. Thousand Oaks, CA: Sage Publications, 2001.

Cullinane, Jan. *The Single Woman's Guide to Retirement*. Hoboken, NJ: John Wiley & Sons, 2012.

Dychtwald, Ken. *Age Power: How the 21st Century Will Be Ruled by the New Old*. New York: Tarcher, 2000.

Dychtwald, Ken, and Daniel J. Kadlec. *The Power Years*. Hoboken, NJ: John Wiley & Sons, 2005.

Dychtwald, Ken, and Daniel J. Kadlec. *A New Purpose: Redefining Money, Family, Work, Retirement, and Success*. New York: HarperCollins, 2009.

Frankel, Bruce. *What Should I Do with the Rest of My Life? True Stories of Finding Success, Passion, and New Meaning in the Second Half of Life*. New York: Avery, 2010.

Freedman, Marc. *Prime Time: How Baby Boomers Will Revolutionize Retirement and Transform America*. New York: Perseus, 1999.

———. *Encore: Finding Work that Matters in the Second Half of Life*. New York: PublicAffairs, 2014.

Freudenheim, Ellen. *Looking Forward: An Optimist's Guide to Retirement*. New York: Stewart, Tabori & Chang, 2004.

Goldman, Connie, and Richard Mahler. *Secrets of a Late Bloomer: Staying Creative, Aware, and Involved in Midlife and Beyond*. Minneapolis: Fairview Press, 1995.

Goodman, Miriam. *Reinventing Retirement: 389 Ideas about Family, Friends, Health, What to Do and Where to Live*. San Francisco: Chronicle Books, 2008.

Hamm, Allen. *How to Plan for Long-Term Care*. N.p.: Plan Ahead, Inc., 2012.

Hannon, Kerry. *Great Jobs for Everyone 50+: Finding Work That Keeps You Happy and Healthy ... and Pays the Bills*. Hoboken, NJ: John Wiley & Sons, 2017.

Jenkins, Jo Ann and Boe Workman. *Disrupt Aging: A Bold New Path to Living Your Best Life at Every Age*. New York: PublicAffairs, 2016.

Johnson, Richard P. *What Color is Your Retirement?* Self-published, 2006.

Jones, Karen. *Death for Beginners*. Self-published, 2010.

Kinder, George. *The Seven Stages of Money Maturity: Understanding the Spirit and Value of Money in Your Life*. New York: Dell Publishing, 1999.

Klinenberg, Eric. *Going Solo: The extraordinary rise and surprising appeal of living alone*. New York: Penguin, 2012.

Kübler-Ross, Elisabeth. *On Death and Dying*. New York: Scribner, 1997.

Leider, Richard J. *The Power of Purpose: Find Meaning, Live Longer, Better*. San Francisco: Berrett-Koehler, 2015.

Leider, Richard J., and Alan Webber. *Life Reimagined: Discovering Your New Life Possibilities*. San Francisco: Berrett-Koehler, 2013.

Leider, Richard J., and David A Shapiro. *Repacking Your Bags: Lighten Your Load for the Good Life*. San Francisco: Berrett-Koehler, 2012.

Live Smart After 50: The Experts' Guide to Life Planning for Uncertain Times. Edited by Life Planning Network. Self-published, 2013.

MacKay, Carleen. *Plan B for Boomers*. San Diego, CA: San Diego Workforce Partnership, 2009.

Moody, Harry R. *Aging: Concepts and Controversies*. Thousand Oaks, CA: Pine Forge Press, 2010.

Newhouse, Meg. (2016) *Legacies of the Heart: Living a Life That Matters*. Self-published, 2016.

Not Your Mother's Retirement. Edited by Mark Evan Chimsky. Self-published by the editor, 2014.

Orman, Suze. *Suze Orman's Action Plan: New Rules for New Times*. New York: Spiegel & Grau, 2010.

The Oxford Book of Aging. Edited by Thomas R. Cole and Mary G Winkler. Oxford: Oxford Univ. Press, 1994.

Rentsch, Gail, and The Transition Network. *Smart Women Don't Retire—They Break Free*. New York: Springboard Press, 2008.

Sadler, William A., and James H. Krefft. *Changing Course: How to Create the Life You Want*. N.p.: Center for Third Age Leadership Press, 2007.

Sedlar, Jeri, and Rick Miners. *Don't Retire, Rewire!: 5 Steps to Fulfilling Work That Fuels Your Passion, Suits Your Personality, and Fills Your Pocket*, 2nd ed. New York: Alpha Books, 2007.

Seligman, Martin E. P. *Authentic Happiness*. New York: Free Press, 2002.

———. *How to Change Your Mind and Your Life*. New York: Pocket Books, 1998.

Stone, Marika, and Howard Stone. *Too Young to Retire: 101 Ways to Start the Rest of Your Life*. New York: Plume, 2004.

Taylor, Roberta, and Dorian Mintzer *The Couple's Retirement Puzzle: 10 Must-Have Conversations for Creating an Amazing New Life Together*. Naperville, IL: Sourcebooks, 2014.

Thomas, Bill. *Second Wind: Navigating the Passage to a Slower, Deeper, and More Connected Life.* New York: Simon & Schuster, 2014.

Vaillant, George E. *Aging Well: Surprising Guideposts to a Happier Life from the Landmark Harvard Study of Adult Development.* New York: Little Brown, 2002.

Wendel, Richard G. *Retire with a Mission: Planning and Purpose for the Second Half of Life.* Self-published, 2008.

Zelinski, Emie. *How to Retire Happy, Wild and Free: Retirement Wisdom That You Won't Get from Your Financial Advisor.* Edmonton, Alberta: Visions International Publishing, 2009.

ACKNOWLEDGMENTS

Essential Retirement Planning for Solo Agers could not have been written without tremendous encouragement and support.

Mary Wayne Bush, Andrea Gallagher, Jan Hively, Sandi Kane, and Sharon Nichols read my initial draft and gave me valuable suggestions for additions and new directions. You gave me the encouragement that kept me moving forward.

Avis Brown, Linda Cayot, Esther Erman, Carol Piras, Donna Schafer, Jan Seamons, Eileen Sheridan, and Deena Zacharin spent hours reading and commenting on the second draft and gave me valuable input and suggestions. I was awed by your support and encouragement of this work.

Linda Baxter, a friend and published author, taught me how to edit my own book, so that when it went to the professionals, it was already a much stronger work. David Colin Carr and Lily O'Brien, professional editors, gave me editing tips and guidance on an early draft, well beyond what I paid them for.

I want to specially thank Kaye Sharbrough, founder of Senior Seasons, for helping me better understand the many different kinds of residential communities available to older adults today. And I want to thank Maggie Brothers, attorney-at-law in Santa Rosa, CA, for helping me write an accurate guide for care and estate planning, and for allowing me to use her well-crafted chart, "Estate Planning, Who Does What and When," in Chapter 22. My thanks, also, to Dorian Mintzer who helped me sort out the resources I needed for publication.

By the time the book reached 70,000 words, my husband, Chuck, and my dear friend Mary Wayne Bush took the time to read the entire final draft and give me the ultimate push to get it into shape for a publisher's eye. I love you both dearly for your contribution to this effort.

I also want to thank Brenda Knight, my editor at Mango Publishing. She believed in this book from the start and shepherded it through the twists and turns of the publishing process. For a first-time author, this was invaluable.

To the many people I interviewed for your stories: I am so grateful for the contribution you made to this book. It would be a far duller read without the color of your lives and experiences.

ABOUT THE AUTHOR

Sara Zeff Geber is a certified retirement coach and professional speaker. She is a recognized expert in planning for the next stage of life, providing knowledge and tools to help people fifty years old and over to better prepare for the future—retirement and beyond. She speaks at meetings, conferences, singles clubs, senior centers, and professional organizations where people are interested in helping themselves and others make successful transitions to the next stage of life.

Sara has made raising awareness of the special challenges of Solo Agers her personal crusade, speaking and writing to financial planners, gerontology professionals, developers, lawmakers, and others who play a role in the aging of America.

Sara has a PhD in Counseling and Organizational Behavior, an MA in Guidance and Counseling, and a BA in Psychology. Before shifting her focus to retirement and aging, Sara was a leadership and organizational consultant, working with organizations and individuals to be more effective in work and in life.

Sara was a contributing author to Live Smart After 50: The Experts' Guide to Planning for Uncertain Times (2013) and a chapter author for Not Your Mother's Retirement (2014).

A native of the San Francisco Bay Area, Sara is an active member of the Life Planning Network (LPN) and is a founding member of the NorCal chapter of LPN. She is a member of The Transition Network, the American Society on Aging, and AARP, and she is an active participant in the Positive Aging movement. She lives with her husband and their canine companion in Santa Rosa, California. She and her husband actively build and nurture their own social networks and continue to pursue all the recommendations in this book.

CPSIA information can be obtained
at www.ICGtesting.com
Printed in the USA
JSHW031540090723
44431JS00002B/2